THE Holocaust

Editor
Geoffrey Wigoder

A
Grolier Student
Library

Volume 2
Family Camps to Lvov

Grolier Educational

SHERMAN TURNPIKE, DANBURY, CONNECTICUT

Concept, Content and Editorial Advisor
Charles E. Smith

Managing Editor
Rachel Gilon

Library of Congress Cataloging-in-Publication Data

The Holocaust.
    p.   cm.
  Summary. Articles identify and describe individuals and events connected with the persecution of Jews and others across Europe in the 1930s and 1940s.
  ISBN 0-7172-7637-6
  1. Holocaust , Jewish (1939-1945)—Encyclopedias, Juvenile.
[1. Holocaust , Jewish (1939-1945)—Encyclopedias.]
D804.25.H65 1996
940.53'18'03—dc20

                                       96-9566
                                        CIP
                                        AC

Published 1997 by Grolier Educational,
Sherman Turnpike, Danbury, Connecticut
© 1997 by Charles E. Smith Books, Inc.

Set ISBN 0-7172-7637-6
Volume 2: ISBN 0-7172-7639-2

For information, address the publisher:
Grolier Educational, Sherman Turnpike, Danbury, Connecticut 06816

Cover design by Smart Graphics
Planned and produced by The Jerusalem Publishing House, Jerusalem
Printed in Hong Kong

f

FAMILY CAMPS

Camps established in forests in eastern Europe by Jewish men, women and children taking refuge from Nazi capture.

From the summer of 1942 through the first half of 1943, the JEWS of western Belarus (see BYELORUSSIA) and western UKRAINE were being massacred. Tens of thousands of Jews managed to flee to the forests, where they formed camps, ranging in size from tens of families to much larger. The camp of Tuvia BIELSKI in the Naliboki forest of western Belarus, for example, contained 1,200 people. The families continued hiding until the liberation of the region by the Russians in July 1944.

In a debate between Tuvia Bielski and the Jewish freedom fighter, Baruch Levin, on where their priorities should be—the struggle against the Germans or the protection of the family camps—Bielski said: "I would like you to know one thing. Since so few of us are left, it is important for me that Jews should remain alive. I see this as the essence of the matter."

From Rescue Attempts during the Holocaust, Jerusalem: Yad Vashem, 1977, p.348.

The "family camp" of the Bielski brothers in the Naliboki Forest, Byelorussia

The camps were uniquely self-reliant, receiving virtually no help from outside. The families were protected by armed members of the camp who had the additional responsibility of providing food. This often meant carrying out raids in villages close to the forest, leading to clashes with police, local non-Jewish partisans and the local peasants themselves. These raids were dangerous and lives were lost. While necessary to provide for the survival of the families, the raids antagonized the already antisemitic Ukrainian population. Local villagers often led the Germans to the family camps, resulting in wholesale slaughter. Along with the dangers of climate and disease, the camps could not guarantee the safety of their families. Estimates are that less than 10,000 Jews were saved in this way.

By 1943, Jewish partisans were actively striking at the Germans and retreating to the same forests which sheltered the families. This created two problems for the families. First, as the Germans hunted the partisans, they found the camps. Second, the partisans sought the participation of the armed men in the camps in the struggle against the Germans, which left the camps unprotected. For these reasons, some of the Jewish partisans had a negative attitude toward the family camps.

FAREYNEGTE PARTIZANER ORGANIZATSYE (FPO)

("United Fighters' Organization")

UNDERGROUND Jewish organization set up on 21 January 1942, inside the VILNA GHETTO. Its goal was to fight the Germans and especially to defend ghetto residents against being killed. Its first leader was Yitzhak WITTENBERG.

Members of this organization were constantly on the move: sabotaging trains and industrial sites, forging documents to help fellow Jews, and searching far and wide for arms and ammunition, which they smuggled into the ghetto. Their attempts to link up with Polish underground fighters was not successful. The FPO soon become involved in a bitter conflict with the ghetto JUDENRAT, the local Jewish Council set up by the Germans.

The Judenrat's chairman was Jacob GENS, a good administrator who saw to it that the Vilna ghetto ran smoothly. Gens thought that the FPO and its activities threatened the lives of the ghetto residents. Gens had a role in handing over Wittenberg to the Germans.

After Wittenberg's escape, the Germans threatened to kill all the Jews of the ghetto unless he gave

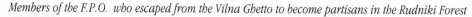

Members of the F.P.O. who escaped from the Vilna Ghetto to become partisans in the Rudniki Forest

himself up. The FPO was ready to fight to defend its leader, but Gens, backed by most of those in the ghetto, pressured its members not to. Wittenberg surrendered on 16 July 1943, and later committed suicide or was murdered by the Germans.

Abba KOVNER was then elected to take over the FPO. He immediately began preparations to move the fighters out of the ghetto and into the forests. A first group of PARTISANS left for the forest on 24 July, but they were ambushed by the Germans. The Nazis "punished" those who had remained in the ghetto so severely that the FPO halted further moves to the forest. In September, the Nazis decided to liquidate the ghetto. The FPO tried to fight and successfully stood up to the Germans on two occasions. However, most of the population was against the fighting and wanted to be evacuated, not realizing that they were to be sent to DEATH CAMPS.

Eventually, the remaining partisans—numbering approximately 500 to 700—escaped from the ghetto through the sewers. They regrouped in the forests, some later joining Soviet partisan movements. A number of FPO fighters took part in the liberation of Vilna by the Soviet army the following year, on 13 July 1944.

FASCISM AND FASCIST MOVEMENTS

Terms for a range of extreme right-wing movements sharing similar beliefs about power in government. The word fascism comes from the Italian word, *fascio,* meaning "a bundle of rods with an axe." This was a symbol of state power in ancient Rome, which stood for the strength of the many, united and obeying one will. The term fascism was first used in 1919 in ITALY by Benito MUSSOLINI, who laid down that it was the opposite of democracy and the liberal ideals of the French Revolution.

Fascist movements appeared in most countries in Europe during the time between the two world wars (1918–1938). Fascism emerged among the discontented. The economic crises of the 1920s and 1930s were important factors, while hatred and fear of communism were another. People who were disillusioned with liberal democracies and felt that their problem could be solved by a strong leader,

flocked to its banner. Fascism achieved power in SPAIN under General Francisco Franco in 1936–1939. In the 1930s, it also spread outside Europe. It played an important role in two countries: JAPAN and ARGENTINA. Although there were variations in these movements in different places, all called for extreme patriotism, militarism, and RACISM. They used rallies, uniforms, paramilitary displays, and street violence to promote their aims of overthrowing the existing society. They glorified military heroes, military values and past events, and were held together by charismatic leaders. Fascist movements usually drew their support from the lower-middle and middle classes. Sometimes they were also backed by landowners, industrialists, the army, and the civil service.

German Nazism was the most deadly and destructive of all fascist movements and regimes. It linked German striving for national rebirth with a radical racism, which was directed mostly at the Jews. Under Adolf HITLER's charismatic leadership, Nazi radicals took complete control of the German state and legal system. From this position of power, they turned their aggressive foreign policy into world war, and their radical policy of antisemitism into the HOLOCAUST. During WORLD WAR II, fascist parties were in power in many countries under German control. They were the natural partners of the Nazis, whose backing brought them to power in countries such as ROMANIA, HUNGARY and CROATIA.

Fascism became relatively unpopular by the end of World War II. However, it is still able to inspire neo-fascist groups today. In most cases, these groups are marginal, but they are to be found in many countries (SEE NEO-NAZISM).

FILMS, NAZI ANTISEMITIC

Films were an important part of the PROPAGANDA of the Nazis, so they naturally expressed their ANTISEMITISM through this medium. In 1939, they produced two comedies to make fun of the JEWS.

Three major anti-Jewish films were made in 1940. The theme of *The Rothschilds* was "While nations bleed on the killing fields, the Jew speculates on the stock market." The plot is supposedly based on the history of the famous Rothschild family of bankers, which was originally from GERMANY. In fact,

Poster for the Nazi antisemitic film "Der ewige Jude," (The Eternal Jew)

the film's story is false and slanderous. It depicts Jews as wealthy aristocrats and greedy parasites. The film was a failure and was only shown for a short period. *Jew Süss* was based on the story of an actual eighteenth-century Jewish banker who was advisor to a German ruler. He is portrayed as a horrible character who rapes an "Aryan" woman. She then drowns herself in despair. In the end, Jew Süss is executed. All the Jews in the film are shown as terrible people. Heinrich HIMMLER issued an order that this film had to be seen by the entire SS and police forces. It was frequently shown to CONCENTRATION CAMP guards. *The Eternal Jew* was the most dreadful of these films. Unlike the others, it was presented in the form of an "authentic" documentary. It represented the Jews as loathsome pests by interchanging pictures of Jews with pictures of rats. It ended with a supposed film of a ritual murder, based on the medieval lie that Jews killed Christian children at Passover time to use their blood. This film was also shown to Nazi personnel engaged in killing Jews. It served to strengthen the killers' beliefs that

December 14, 1942

I went to see the film Jew Süss. What I saw there made my blood boil. I was red in the face when I came out. I realized there the wicked objectives of these evil people—how they want to inject the poison of antisemitism into the blood of the gentiles. While I was watching the film I suddenly remembered what the evil one [Hitler] had said in one of his speeches: "Whichever side wins the war, antisemitism will spread and spread until the Jews are no more." In that film I saw the means he is using to achieve his aim. And if nothing happens to counteract his work, then surely the poison will spread in people's blood. The way in which jealousy, hatred and loathing are aroused is simply indescribable. One thing I know if we are not saved now by some miracle from heaven, then our end is as sure as I am sitting here. For not only the body of Israel is being attacked, but also its spirit. The Jews are being made so hateful to the world that nothing that anyone can do will be able to undo his work. When I left the cinema, I realized the nature of the fiend and I knew what I had to do, if—God willing—I can attain my objective.

In the film, Jew Süss says to a young girl: "We too have a God, but this God is the Lord of Vengeance." This is a lie, pure and simple. Our Lord is the same Lord who said: "Love thy neighbor as thyself," but now I pray He may appear as a "Lord of vengeance."

from Young Moshe's Diary by Moshe Flinker, a 16-year-old boy who was living in Brussels, Belgium

their victims were less than human and to condition them for their murderous work.

FILMS ON THE HOLOCAUST

The unique nature of the HOLOCAUST has led many film makers to treat the subject. The making of films

Films on the Holocaust

Au Revoir les Enfants (1987, director: Louis Malle). The French director based this film on his childhood memory of a Jewish boy, hidden in a Catholic school in France, who is turned over for deportation to his death.

The Diary of Anne Frank (1959, director: George Stevens). The story of the Frank family's years in hiding in Holland before discovery and deportation to the camps.

Europa Europa (1991, director: Agnieszka Holland). A powerful drama based on the true story of a Jewish boy who survived the Holocaust, disguised as a Hitler Youth member.

The Garden of the Finzi Continis (1970, director: Vittorio De Sica). A melancholy study of the doom that gradually overtakes a wealthy Jewish family in Italy during the Holocaust.

The Great Dictator (1940). Charlie Chaplin wrote, directed and played in this film. In fact he plays two characters: the dictator, a satire on Adolf Hitler, and a poor Jewish barber.

Holocaust (1978, director: Marvin Chomsky). A television mini-series centered on the fictional Weiss family, of which each member represents a different aspect of the Jewish Holocaust experience.

Judgment at Nuremberg (1961, director: Stanley Kramer). A fictionalized version of the Nuremberg trial of Nazi judges that poses probing questions about guilt and responsibility.

Night and Fog (1955, director: Alain Resnais). A landmark documentary view of the concentration camp.

The Pawnbroker (1965, director: Sidney Lumet). A drama about a Holocaust survivor tormented by his memories while trying to cope with the violence surrounding him in New York.

Schindler's List (1994, director: Steven Spielberg). Probably the highest-profiled of all Holocaust-related feature films, dealing with the real-life drama of the German businessman and playboy Oskar Schindler. Schindler used his commercial interests in Nazi-occupied Poland as a cover for saving his Jewish workers.

Shoah (1985, director: Claude Lanzmann). A classic 9-hour reconstruction, through contemporary interviews, of the details involved in the "Final Solution."

The Shop on Main Street (1965). A Czech film about an old Jewish woman trying to survive under the Nazis.

Sophie's Choice (1982). Based on a book by William Styron, Meryl Streep plays a Polish woman who survives Nazi Europe and struggles with terrible memories in her later life in the United States.

The Sorrow and the Pity (1970, director: Marcel Ophuls). A documentary by the French director Marcel Ophuls, which reveals how French people often cooperated with the German persecution of the Jews or closed their eyes to it.

The Tin Drum (1979, director: Volker Schlondorff). The screen version of Günter Grass's novel about a dwarf boy who refuses to continue growing under Nazi rule in Germany.

on the Holocaust does not appear to have slowed with the passage of time. It has rather taken on increased importance as first-hand memories of the period become fewer. The most important films that portray what happened do not date from the immediate postwar period, but from four or five decades later.

Genuine film records of actual killings are almost non-existent. These are limited to amateur footage of mass shootings photographed by German soldiers. The many documentaries produced on the subject have thus always faced a problem: how to fill the gap between the newsreel images of prewar persecution and the horrors documented by the Allied armies that liberated the CONCENTRATION CAMPS. The French director Alain Resnais's *Night and Fog*

(1955), an early serious film, shows black and white 1945 concentration camp footage and color scenes filmed in the same locations a decade later. Another Frenchman, Claude Lanzmann, in his outstanding 9-hour *Shoah* (1985), made no use of archive material. It portrays the process of the killing solely through contemporary interviews with those who lived through the experience, on both sides.

Feature films, which do not rely on actual filmed footage, also rarely show the mass murders themselves. It is not realistic to try to convey the impact of millions of deaths. In addition, there are moral and ethical problems connected to presenting the circumstances in which so many people were murdered. Polish director Wanda Jakubowska's *The Last Stage* (1948), gave a first-hand view of AUSCHWITZ where she herself survived the war. Most features have concentrated on individual stories. The fate of the individual is the most powerful way to convey the impact of the Holocaust.

In GERMANY, one of the first of this type of film was Wolfgang Staudte's *The Murderers are Among Us* (1947). It deals with the guilt of a doctor who had witnessed the crimes of his countrymen. During the war, Hollywood directors Charles Chaplin and Ernst Lubitsch had ridiculed the Nazis in *The Great Dictator* (1940) and *To Be or Not to Be* (1942). It took Hollywood longer to come to grips with the deeper issues. *The Diary of Anne Frank* brought the story of Anne FRANK to the screen as a major motion picture under the direction of George Stevens in 1959. The Jewish identity of the victims is played down in both this film and Stanley Kramer's *Judgment at Nuremberg* (1961). This has continued to be true of many later films. One exception was Sidney Lumet's *The Pawnbroker* (1965), whose main character's mind was permanently scarred by his treatment at the hands of the Nazis.

In 1978, an ambitious attempt was made to capture the entire range of wartime Jewish experiences in Europe in the television mini-series, *Holocaust*. While criticized as being shallow and like a soap opera, it was widely seen and stimulated new interest in the subject. Two more recent successful films have further increased the general public's awareness of the Holocaust. Agnieszka Holland's *Europa Europa* (1991) is based on the true story of Salomon Perel, who survived the war masquerading

as a member of the HITLER YOUTH. Steven Spielberg's *Schindler's List* (1994) is based on Thomas Keneally's book about Oskar SCHINDLER, who used his wartime manufacturing plant in POLAND to save the lives of hundreds of Jews. This film in particular, brought knowledge of the Holocaust to an especially large audience because of the director's reputation as a successful producer of entertainment.

FINAL SOLUTION

The "Final Solution" (to the Jewish Problem) was the Nazis' code-term for the decision to kill all the Jews of Europe.

The Nazis deliberately did not use the word "murder" to name their chilling plan. Yet there was a certain exactness to the term they chose. Final meant forever. By killing all the JEWS they would be solving the "Jewish problem"—the existence of Jews—for all time.

Some historians claim that the Nazis had intended from the very beginning to murder all the Jews of Europe. Others believe that this decision was taken only after two earlier policies had failed. The first had been the forced emigration of Jews, which did not work because no nation wanted to receive Jews. The second was the forced removal of Jews to a place where they could be isolated, such as the island of MADAGASCAR (off the coast of Africa).

Still, all agree that the "Final Solution" was a secret German policy from 22 June 1941—the date of the invasion of the SOVIET UNION. It became an announced policy from 20 January 1942, when senior officials were informed of the decision at the WANNSEE CONFERENCE.

FINLAND

Country in the eastern part of Scandinavia. Finland admitted 250 Jewish REFUGEES from Central Europe in the 1930s. After refusing to cooperate with demands from SOVIET RUSSIA, Finland was attacked by Russian forces in November 1939. The small Jewish community of 2,000 answered the call to arms and many of its members served in the Finnish army. After a brave defense lasting several months, Finland surrendered in March 1940 and was forced to give

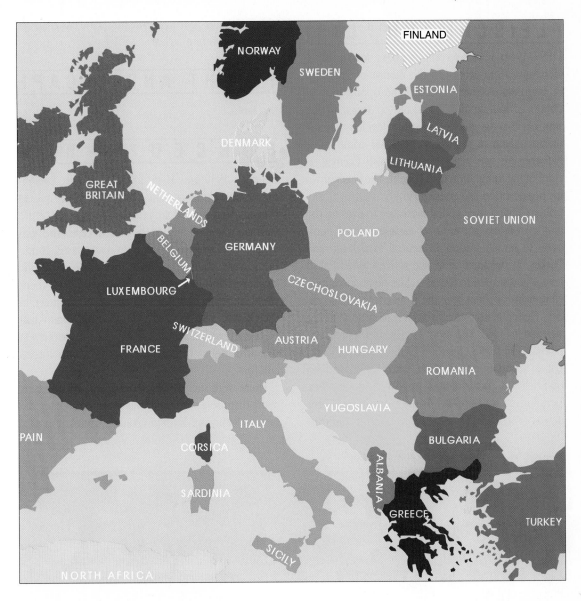

up territory to Russia, including the city of Vipurii (Vyborg). The Jews of that city, together with other Finns, were evacuated to other areas in Finland.

In 1941, Finland allied itself with GERMANY in an attempt to regain its lost territories. Despite that, the Jews kept their equal status. Although Germany demanded that Finland surrender its Jewish community, the Finnish authorities refused. Prime Minister Johann Wilhelm Rangell was reported to have told Heinrich HIMMLER when he came to Finland that the Jews of Finland were "decent people and loyal citizens whose sons fought in the army like other Finns. We have no Jewish question here." Jews even served in the Finnish army alongside German units

during the siege of Leningrad and elsewhere. Twenty-three lost their lives in the fighting. In 1943, however, eight Jewish refugees were deported to Germany (only one survived).

There were protests by Finland's minority Social Democratic Party and by the Lutheran archbishop and other ministers of that church. As a result, the Finnish government refused to hand over any other Jews to the Germans. Marshal Carl Gustaf von Mannerheim, the country's wartime leader, also showed his opposition to antisemitic German demands. In December 1944, he attended a memorial service at Helsinki's synagogue for the Jewish soldiers who had fallen in battle.

FLEISCHMANN, GISI

(1897–1944) Jewish Slovak RESISTANCE leader. Fleischmann was an activist in the Zionist organization in Bratislava. As such, she had the opportunity to obtain an immigration certificate to PALESTINE. She sent her two daughters there, but decided that she would remain in SLOVAKIA to help her community. Fleischmann was active in the Jewish Council as chief of the emigration department. She was known for her devotion and courage.

Fleischmann used coded messages to pass on the first eyewitness accounts of escapees from DEATH CAMPS to Jewish leaders in neutral SWITZERLAND and Turkey. At the same time, she actively aided Polish Jews who escaped to Slovakia. She helped in smuggling many of them over the Slovak-Hungarian border. Fleischmann herself traveled to HUNGARY in an attempt to win support for the EUROPA PLAN—a scheme for saving Jews by bribing Nazi officials. These negotiations, however, were broken off on Heinrich HIMMLER's order in August 1943. In 1944, Fleischmann was arrested by the Germans and sent to AUSCHWITZ with the instructions, "return undesir-able." She was sent to her death in the GAS CHAMBERS immediately upon arrival.

FLIGHT AND ESCAPE

see BERIHA.

FORCED LABOR

Between 1939 and 1945, millions of JEWS, prisoners of war, other civilians, and CONCENTRATION CAMP inmates were forced to work in the service of the German war economy. In the best of cases, the conditions were extremely harsh. In many cases, conditions were so horrible that the workers quickly weakened and died. By the summer of 1944, there were approximately 7.8 million forced workers in the German war economy. By this time, nearly half of all farm workers and one-third of the workers in the armaments industry in GERMANY were forced laborers.

There were such severe shortages of labor in Germany that the government was required to use prisoners of war and foreign civilians from the begin-

Jews selected for forced labor, Bratislava, c1940

ning of the war. Most of these worked at first in agriculture. The main increase in foreign workers came after the winter of 1941–1942. By that time, the length of the war, which had begun in 1939, was weakening the German work force. The Nazis then began mass DEPORTATIONS of Soviet prisoners of war and civilians to Germany for forced labor. As a result, 2.8 million Soviet citizens alone were working in Germany by June 1944. Finally, as the Germans became more and more desperate, hundreds of thousands of concentration camp inmates were also put to work in German factories in 1944.

While the western European workers had a harsh but tolerable standard of living, the eastern Europeans, especially Poles and Soviet citizens, were treated in a shockingly inhuman fashion. Worst of all was the treatment of concentration camp inmates and Jews.

Hundreds of thousands of Jews were sent by the ORGANIZATION TODT, the army, industry, and the SS to large-scale road-building, construction projects, and armaments manufacturing. Many were worked to death under appalling conditions. For others it merely increased their suffering prior to their even-

tual murder. For some, working in an armaments factory allowed them to survive—indeed, many Jews volunteered for forced labor in the hope that they might survive in this way.

Most Jewish forced labor took place in POLAND. However, this was seen as a temporary measure by the SS. In 1943, industry and the army came under increasing pressure to release their Jewish workers for deportation to DEATH CAMPS. Most were eventually killed.

Jews in the satellite countries of eastern Europe were also sent to forced labor. In BULGARIA they were forced to build roads. Jews from ROMANIA were sent to TRANSNISTRIA and condemned to forced labor. In HUNGARY they were turned over to the Germans to build fortifications.

F O R T   N I N E

The last of nine forts built around the city of KOVNO in LITHUANIA. The forts were built towards the end of the nineteenth century, as defenses for the Russian Empire. During Lithuania's independence (1818–1939), the forts served as arsenals, ware-

Women performing forced labor at Ravensbrück camp, Germany

(left and right) Fort Nine, site of massacre of Jews in Kovno, Lithuania

houses, and prisons. Fort Nine is located four miles north of Kovno.

Soon after the German invasion of SOVIET RUSSIA (June 1941) Fort Nine was chosen as a possible CONCENTRATION CAMP for Kovno's JEWS. On 26 September 1941, the first 1,000 Jews were taken there. A hundred more, including infants, were taken there on 4 October. On that same day, 1,845 Jews (including 712 women and 818 CHILDREN) were shot.

Fort Nine was the site of one of the largest mass shootings of Jews in the Holocaust. On 28 October 1941, 9,200 Kovno GHETTO Jews—2,007 men, 2,900 women, and 4,273 children—were "selected" (see SELEKTIONEN) by the GESTAPO commander for death. They were marched to Fort Nine the next day, stripped of their clothes, pushed into trenches dug by previous prisoners, and shot.

The Germans used Fort Nine as a killing center for Jews deported from central Europe and as far away as southern FRANCE. Jews were murdered there as late as 1944. As the Soviet army began to approach Lithuania in 1943, the German authorities tried to destroy evidence of the murders. The masses of bodies were dug up (a steam shovel was put into use), and a group of prisoners was forced to burn the bodies.

Very few of those taken to Fort Nine lived very long after. In December 1943, however, 64 prisoners who were at work digging up and burning bodies, successfully escaped the fort. Nineteen reached the Kovno ghetto, where they were hidden until they could be smuggled into the surrounding forests. The rest were recaptured by the Germans.

It is estimated that 50,000 to 70,000 people were killed at Fort Nine. In 1984, on the 40th anniversary of the liberation of Kovno, the Soviet government dedicated a monument to the SOVIET PRISONERS OF WAR and citizens killed there. In 1991, additional monuments were set up as memorials to the Jewish dead.

FORT ONTARIO

"Emergency refugee shelter" established by the United States government in 1944 in Oswego, New York.

In 1944, various Jewish organizations, relief agencies, and well-known journalists pressured the U.S. government to create temporary CAMPS for European REFUGEES. In May, John W. PEHLE, the Executive Director of the newly created WAR REFUGEE BOARD discussed the issue with U.S. President Franklin D. ROOSEVELT. Roosevelt was sympathetic, but fearing that a large influx of refugees would arouse anti-immigration sentiment in Congress and in the general public, limited the number of incoming refugees to 1,000. On 8 June, Roosevelt made known his decision to create an "emergency refugee shelter" at Fort Ontario. The War Refugee Board was given overall charge of the project, while the War Relocation Authority was to handle the day-to-day operations. Four days later, Roosevelt announced the plan to Congress and assured its members that at the end of the war the refugees would be returned to their "homelands."

Shortly after the decision was made, 982 refugees were selected from a pool of 3,000 potential candidates held in internment camps in southern Italy. As the president had requested, the refugees chosen

Eleanor Roosevelt visiting refugees from Europe staying at Fort Ontario, 20 September 1944

were from different ethnic groups and religions. The largest groups came from YUGOSLAVIA (369), AUSTRIA (237), POLAND (146), and GERMANY (96). Eight hundred and seventy four of these were Jews and about 100 had been prisoners in DACHAU or BUCHENWALD.

The refugees left Italy aboard an American troopship, and sailed into New York harbor on 3 August. Two days later, they arrived at Fort Ontario, a former U.S. army base in Oswego, an upstate New York town with a population of about 22,000.

During the shelter's eighteen-month existence, the residents faced difficulties. It was difficult to adjust to the new surroundings and wartime restrictions created tensions. Rivalries among the people from different nationalities also caused friction. Residents were not permitted to come and go as they pleased, and that became a major source of despair. They were confined to the fort. For the first month of their stay. In September, the restrictions loosened up a little so that they could visit Oswego, receive visitors, and attend the local schools. During the harsh winter of 1944–1945, residents became increasingly discouraged over their internment.

As the war drew to a close, the Fort Ontario refugees became uncertain of their future. Most did not want to return to their "homelands" and requested to stay in the United States. In the summer and fall of 1945, 69 inhabitants of Fort Ontario voluntarily left the country, mainly for Yugoslavia. On 22 December, U.S. President Harry S. TRUMAN, decided to depart from Roosevelt's conditions. He ordered the Secretary of State and the Attorney General to change the immigration status of the Fort Ontario residents so that those who wanted to remain in the country could do so under the existing laws. In early 1946, the refugees left Oswego for the U.S. Consul's office in Niagara Falls, CANADA. There they received visas allowing them to enter the United States as immigrants. They then crossed the border and began new lives in the United States.

FOSTER HOMES

By 1942, when JEWS were being murdered throughout Europe, Jewish parents had to make very difficult choices in an effort to save their children. Thousands chose to put them into hiding with non-Jews. Often, the people who hid these children were strangers. Separated from their parents, the children were alone and frightened. They had to take on new identities and live in secret for months or years. Non-Jewish families hid children in barns, fields, closets, attics, between walls, and even in sewers. Many children were also hidden in convents and monasteries. Due to the size of religious institutions, they were able to hide larger numbers than individual families. No matter where these children were, they were never totally safe. They could be betrayed, even by neighbors. Frequently, children were moved from place to place.

For some Jewish children, hiding in convents and monasteries meant giving up their Jewishness. Playing their new roles as Christian children was very confusing. While they continued to cling to the memories of their parents and families, Judaism became for them a religion of danger, a religion that could not even protect its children. By contrast, Christianity seemed safe and protective.

There was great danger involved for the families who hid Jewish children. These rescuers, who risked their own lives to save Jewish children, came from a wide range of backgrounds. They chose to take this chance for many different reasons. Most were honorable, while some were not. (Some did it for the money they received or with the intention of converting the children to Christianity). In 1953, the Israeli government passed a Martyrs'and Heroes' Remembrance Law that defined those people who risked their lives to save Jews as "RIGHTEOUS AMONG THE NATIONS."

The healing process for adults who lived out the war as hidden children has been difficult. After years of living in hiding, not speaking above a whisper, and taking on false identities, it was hard for these survivors to learn to trust again and to rebuild their lives. After the war, many of these children faced big problems. Some had grown so attached to their foster-families that they did not want to leave them. Some foster-families did want to let the children go. Often children remained in touch with their foster-families for decades to come.

F R A N C E

Country in western Europe. It entered WORLD WAR II in September 1939, together with GREAT BRITAIN. This was after the Germans invaded their ally, POLAND. In May 1940, GERMANY began a massive attack on France. France's armies were defeated in a few weeks. Adolf HITLER entered PARIS to gloat over his victory. The Germans occupied northern France—including Paris, which was home to half the country's JEWS. They put southern France under a puppet government led by World War I hero Marshal Philippe PÉTAIN. This was called the VICHY government, named for the small spa town which became its capital. The Vichy government ruled southern France until November 1942. At that time, the whole of France came under German control. At the time of the fall of France in 1940, the French general Charles DE GAULLE escaped to England where he set up a government in exile. De Gaulle challenged the right of the Vichy government to exist. He established fighting forces which fought alongside the Allies throughout the war.

Over 300,000 Jews were living in France before the invasion. A large number of these were REFUGEES from Germany who had arrived during the 1930's.

Hitler in front of the Eiffel Tower

The Germans immediately applied ANTI-JEWISH LEGISLATION in occupied France. Jews were identified, subject to economic discrimination and put under curfew. From 1942, they had to wear a yellow BADGE. The Germans only had 3,000 soldiers in the occupied area. They needed French cooperation to carry out their decrees. This help was readily available.

Pétain's prime minister, Pierre LAVAL, convinced the Vichy that it should be in total COLLABORATION with the Germans. At first, most anti-Jewish activity of the Vichy government was directed against Jews who were not French citizens or who had only recently become citizens. Under German pressure, the Vichy government set up a special section for Jewish affairs, headed by Xavier VALLAT. His main concern was the ARYANIZATION (taking over) of Jewish

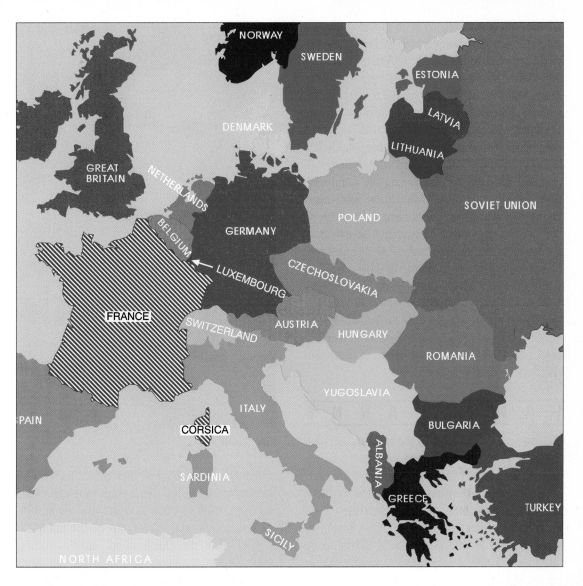

businesses. After a year, he was succeeded by the much more extreme antisemite DARQUIER DE PELLEPOIX. Vichy cooperated closely with the Germans. Many Jews were sent to CONCENTRATION CAMPS. These, including the largest one at DRANCY, were run by the French police.

In July 1942, roundups and DEPORTATIONS began. They continued until 1944. In July 1942, GESTAPO men rounded up 12,000 Jews in the Paris area. In the following month, Vichy police arrested 7,000 foreign Jews and handed them over to the Germans. In the course of many more AKTIONS in both zones, some 80,000 Jews were deported from France. Of these, only 2,000 remained alive at the end of the war.

The southeastern corner of France, including Nice and the southern Alps, was occupied by Italian forces from the summer of 1940 until July 1943. Many Jews who fled there from elsewhere in France found themselves secure in this zone as long as it was ruled by ITALY. However, after that part of France came under the Germans in 1943, many Jews were seized and deported to eastern Europe. Most were gassed on arrival at AUSCHWITZ.

An underground French RESISTANCE movement (*maquis*) was active throughout the war, especially after Germany took over southern France. It was under the leadership of Jean Moulin (who was eventually captured and tortured to death by Klaus BARBIE). Moulin was the representative in France of

General de Gaulle. French Jews played important roles both within the general French resistance movement and within Jewish underground bodies. The Zionist youth organized the ARMÉE JUIVE (Jewish Army) which joined the French scout movement's resistance movement to form the Organisation Juive de Combat (JEWISH FIGHTING ORGANIZATION). The Jewish underground worked actively in organizing the hiding of Jewish CHILDREN. They received considerable support and sympathy for this among the non-Jewish population. On the other hand, there were many Frenchmen who either collaborated in or passively approved of anti-Jewish measures. The extent of French collaboration was hushed-up after the war. It was only formally acknowledged by President Jacques Chirac, 50 years after the end of the war.

When the war ended, the French resistance carried out an informal purge and humiliation of thousands of collaborators. Former leaders Pétain and Laval were tried. Laval was sentenced to death, Pétain to permanent exile.

FRANK, ANNE

(1929–1945) Dutch victim of the HOLOCAUST and author of the famous diary (see DIARIES, HOLOCAUST). Anne Frank and her family left GERMANY for Amsterdam soon after the Nazis seized power in 1933. With the German occupation of the NETHERLANDS in the summer of 1940, Anne's father, Otto Frank, began preparing for the possibility of having to go into hiding. On 5 July 1942, Anne's 16-year-old sister, Margot, received a letter from the Central Office for Jewish Emigration, ordering her to appear for forced labor. The next day the family moved into the vacant annex of Otto's office, with the knowledge and help of some of his employees. A week later they were joined by the family of Otto Frank's partner, Hermann van Daan, and on November 16 an eighth person the dentist Dr. Albert Dussel came to hide in the annex. The small space was very crowded, and food and clothing were difficult to obtain. Otto's employees, however, managed to supply them.

On 4 August 1944, the SD (the security and intelligence service of the SS) in Amsterdam was informed that Jews were in hiding in the annex at Prinsengracht 263 and the eight Jews were found and ar-

Anne Frank

rested. Some of the employees were also arrested and imprisoned in the Netherlands. The eight Jews were sent to the WESTERBORK camp, and from there the Franks were sent to AUSCHWITZ on the last transport to leave the Dutch camp. Anne's mother, Edith, died in Auschwitz, and Anne and her sister were sent to BERGEN-BELSEN, at the end of October 1944. Both died in March 1945 of typhus, shortly before the camp was liberated. Otto Frank survived Auschwitz and lived on until 1980.

Anne had been given a diary for her 13th birthday, on 12 June 1942. She immediately began making entries addressed to her imaginary friend, Kitty. She wrote of her own development, her family relationships, the experience of hiding, the events around her, and her reactions to them. The diary also describes the efforts made by those who hid the Franks to provide for them and protect them. In addition to the diary, Anne wrote stories and a "Book of Beautiful Phrases," full of quotations she liked. After the eight Jews had been arrested, Miep Gies, one of the employees who had helped the

The wall of Anne Frank's room in the Amsterdam hiding place, decorated with her postcards

Dear Kitty,

...We have been pointedly reminded that we are in hiding, that we are Jews in chains.... We Jews mustn't show our feelings, must be brave and strong, must accept all inconveniences and not grumble.... Some time this terrible war will be over. Surely the time will come when we are people again, and not just Jews. Who has inflicted this upon us? Who has made us Jews different from all other people? Who has allowed us to suffer so terribly up till now? It is God that has made us as we are, but it will be God, too, who will raise us up again. If we bear all this suffering and if there are still Jews left, when it is over, then Jews, instead of being doomed, will be held up as an example. Who knows, it might even be our religion from which the world and all peoples learn good, and for that reason and that reason only do we have to suffer now. We can never become just Netherlanders, or just English, or representatives of any country for that matter, we will always remain Jews, but we want to, too. During that night I really felt that I had to die...but now, now I've been saved again, now my first wish after the war is that I may become Dutch!

I don't believe that the big men, the politicians and the capitalists alone are guilty of the war. Oh, no, the little man is just as keen.... There is an urge and rage in the people to destroy, to kill, to murder, and until all mankind, without exception, undergoes a great change, wars will be waged.

April 11, 1944

Franks, took the diary and other papers she found in the annex. When Otto Frank returned from Auschwitz, Gies returned them to him.

In 1947, the diary, under the title *The Annex*, was first published. It has since appeared in over 50 editions, in numerous languages, in roughly 20 million copies. A new expanded and more complete edition was published in 1994. A stage version based on the diary premiered on Broadway on 5 October 1955, and won the Pulitzer Prize for best play of the year. A film version followed in 1959. For many people the diary is their first confrontation with the Nazi persecution of the Jews. Anne Frank has become a symbol of the millions of victims of the Holocaust. The diary has served as a source of inspiration for artists, musicians, and choreographers throughout the world.

In 1960, the annex on Prinsengracht 263 was made into a museum about the struggle against antisemitism and racism (see ANNE FRANK HOUSE). The original diary is on loan to the house from the Anne Frank Foundation, and is on display there. A book of Anne's stories, *Tales From the Secret Annex* (English edition, 1950), was also published.

FRANK, ANNE, HOUSE

see ANNE FRANK HOUSE.

FRANK, HANS

(1900–1946) Nazi governor of POLAND from 1943 to 1945. Frank was a lawyer by profession. He joined the Nazi Party as early as 1923. He was Adolf HITLER's personal lawyer and often appeared in court cases on behalf of the Nazi Party. From October 1930, he headed the law section of the Nazi leadership. He was very ambitious and loyal to Hitler, who was usually suspicious of lawyers.

In 1943, he was appointed governor of the GENERALGOUVERNEMENT, the central region of Poland. Frank was the highest economic and administrative ruler in the region. He was not, however, directly in charge of the murder of the Jews of Poland in the DEATH CAMPS that were built in the area under his rule (see AKTION REINHARD). These were run by the SS and the police. Frank was against the use of his territory as a "racial dumping ground." His objection was not

because of humanitarian reasons—he agreed to the murder of Jews in his territory but was concerned that others had control over a major operation taking place in his region. This was a challenge to his authority. He wrote in one of the 42 volumes of his diary that he had ordered in December 1941, "We must annihilate the Jews, wherever we find them and wherever it is possible, in order to maintain there the structure of the Reich as a whole." At his trial before the International Military Tribunal at Nuremberg (see NUREMBERG TRIAL), he spoke of the guilt that GERMANY had brought upon itself by its actions. He also claimed to have found religion. He was sentenced to death and hanged.

FRANKFURT ON MAIN

City and financial center in western GERMANY. The active Jewish community went back almost 1,000 years before the start of the Nazi period. The Jews of Frankfurt were then relatively well-off. In June 1933, the Jewish population numbered 26,158, making it the second largest Jewish community in Germany (after BERLIN).

Like Jews throughout Germany, Frankfurt Jews suffered Nazi discrimination as soon as the NAZI PARTY came to power in 1933. This included a boycott of Jewish business (see BOYCOTT, ANTI-JEWISH and ANTI-JEWISH LEGISLATION). Many lost jobs in the civil service, professions, and the universities.

In November 1938, during the KRISTALLNACHT pogroms, five large synagogues in Frankfurt were destroyed. Homes and businesses were also burned and looted. On 9-10 November 1938, over 2,000 Frankfurt Jewish men were rounded up and deported to the CONCENTRATION CAMPS of BUCHENWALD and DACHAU. The Frankfurt Rabbinical Academy was also destroyed.

In 1939, the Frankfurt Jewish community was placed under Nazi control. Jewish property was confiscated and financial assets were Aryanized (see ARYANIZATION). Frankfurt's Jewish population had dropped to 10,600 by September 1941, as people fled the country.

The remaining community was almost entirely destroyed during the Holocaust. DEPORTATIONS to the east began on 19 October 1941, when 1,124 Jews were sent to the LÓDZ GHETTO. Over the next four years, further deportations followed to MINSK and

RIGA. All these Jews were sent to their deaths. During August and September 1941, almost 3,000 Jews were deported to THERESIENSTADT. Only some 600 Frankfurt Jews survived the Holocaust.

FRANKFURTER, DAVID

(1909–1982) Assassin of a Nazi leader in SWITZERLAND. Frankfurter was born in Daruvar (CROATIA), the son of an Orthodox rabbi. After beginning his medical studies in GERMANY, he enrolled at the University of Berne, Switzerland, in 1933. Shortly before his final exams he decided to assassinate Wilhelm Gustloff, the leader of the Swiss Nazi Party in Switzerland. Frankfurter entered Gustloff's apartment in the Alpine resort of Davos on 4 February 1936, and shot him dead. In his autobiography, Frankfurter said his main motive for the assassination was the introduction of the NUREMBERG LAWS and other anti-Jewish measures by the Nazis in Germany.

Reactions to the assassination in Switzerland were mostly negative. Even the liberal press and local Jewish communal leaders condemned Frank-

David Frankfurter

furter's act. They thought it would endanger the German Jewish community and be of no help in the battle against Nazi Germany. In Germany, Nazi leaders launched a huge PROPAGANDA campaign to turn the little-known Gustloff into a national martyr. Adolf HITLER himself came to the funeral, where he denounced Frankfurter as part of a world-wide Jewish conspiracy. The Nazis did not, however, respond with active anti-Jewish measures at the time, since the Winter OLYMPIC GAMES OF 1936 were taking place in Germany, and they wanted positive coverage in the world press.

A local Swiss court sentenced Frankfurter to 18 years in prison. The court did not take his political motives into consideration. Jewish and left-wing organizations criticized the verdict. Frankfurter was released from prison after the fall of Nazi Germany in 1945, but was immediately banished from Switzerland. He moved to PALESTINE and worked there as a civil servant. In 1969, the Swiss government lifted the 1945 order that had banished him from Switzerland.

FREEMASONS

A secret fraternity that was persecuted by the Nazis.

The Freemasons were started in 1717. As early as 1732, Jews were admitted into certain Masonic lodges. This was long before JEWS had become accepted in even the most liberal Christian societies. Many antisemites therefore made the link between Freemasons and Jews. They believed Masonic lodges were a cover for a Jewish conspiracy to destroy Christianity. In GERMANY, however, Masonic lodges were themselves antisemitic and few Jews were allowed to become members.

The Nazis held Freemasons to be an ideological enemy. They included all secret brotherhoods in their definition of Freemasons.

Under Nazi rule, Freemasons were at first treated similar to Jews. In 1935, Masonic lodges were dissolved—at first "voluntarily," later by force. Some Freemasons were sent to CONCENTRATION CAMPS. During the KRISTALLNACHT pogroms, SA men were told to paint anti-masonic and antisemitic slogans on stores and synagogues. Over time, however, the Nazi campaign against Freemasons slowed down, since the members were needed to work in the war econ-

A Nazi poster in French showing as enemies: the Freemasons, Jews, and de Gaulle

omy. Partial amnesty was offered to Freemasons who had been dismissed from the civil service. Still, throughout German-occupied Europe, Masonic lodges were closed as the Nazis captured country after country.

FREIKORPS ("Free Corps")

Private armies of former German soldiers who continued to serve under their officers, even after World War I was over. The German Imperial Army was disbanded in 1918. However, the more nationalistic officers formed private armies, which were named in their honor. At first, the Freikorps were secretly armed by the German army. They were used to protect Germany's borders and to put down revolutions at home. By 1919, there were as many as 200 corps with more than 400,000 members.

The members of the Freikorps were made up of unemployed, disappointed soldiers of the defeated German army. In time, many were recruited into the SA and the SS of the rising NAZI PARTY. Interestingly, the Ehrhardt Brigade wore the SWASTIKA symbol on its helmets.

The Freikorps were ordered to disband in 1920. The Nazis treated surviving members of the Freikorps with respect and honor.

FRENCH JEWISH SCOUTS

SEE ECLAIREURS ISRAÉLITES DE FRANCE.

FRY, VARIAN

(1918–1967) First American to be honored as a "RIGHTEOUS AMONG THE NATIONS." Fry was a volunteer in FRANCE with the Emergency Rescue Commission, set up by Eleanor Roosevelt (wife of President Franklin D. ROOSEVELT). He arrived in Marseilles with 200 exit permits for refugees from France. Thousands of persecution victims flooded him with requests for the permits and he decided to forge documents to get more people to freedom.

He was jailed twice but managed to save 4,000 lives, mostly of Jews. Fry was expelled from France in 1941.

Among the lives he saved were artist Marc Chagall, sculptor Jacques Lipchitz, and philosopher Hannah Arendt. In 1996, 31 years after his death, Varian Fry was recognized by YAD YASHEM as a "Righteous among the Nations." A tree was planted in his honor in the Avenue of the Righteous at Yad Vashem by his son together with U.S. Secretary of State Warren Christopher.

FÜHRER, DER ("The Leader")

German title chosen by Adolf HITLER to show his authority when the NAZI PARTY was founded. It later stood for his position as absolute dictator. The title, and the person behind it, assumed almost mystical proportions. With the backing of the Nazi propaganda machine, *Der Führer* was portrayed as a beloved demigod and an example of the most noble qualities that Germans could possess. At major events, people swore oaths of allegiance to *Der Führer*.

Above: U.S. Secretary of State Warren Christopher (right) and James Fry plant a tree at Yad Vashem in Jerusalem in honor of Fry's father, the only U.S. citizen to be named a "Righteous Gentile" for saving Jewish lives during the Holocaust

Below: Adolf Hitler, receiving Benito Mussolini in Germany, 14 June 1934. Both Hitler's title Der Führer and Mussolini's title Il Duce mean "The Leader"

F U N K , W A L T H E R

(1890–1960) Nazi minister of economics. He was a well-known, early follower of the Nazis and a member of the NAZI PARTY from 1930. Funk was involved in various corrupt businesses. He played the important role of attracting industrial and business leaders to the Nazi Party.

Funk became minister of economics in 1938 and president of the Bank of Germany in 1939. He actively supported anti-Jewish economic programs. Following an agreement he made with Heinrich HIMMLER in 1942, valuables belonging to murdered or imprisoned Jews were sent to the Bank of Germany. These included gold teeth and fillings. In 1939 Funk reported that two billion marks worth of German-Jewish property had been seized. Funk was also involved in the use of slave labor and the seizure of wealth in the Nazi-occupied territories. Later in the war, Albert SPEER, Germany's minister of armaments and war production, became more powerful and Funk's importance lessened. At the NUREMBERG TRIAL, Funk was sentenced to life imprisonment, but was released on grounds of ill health in 1957.

Walther Funk (center) and on the right, Albert Speer, German minister of armaments and war production

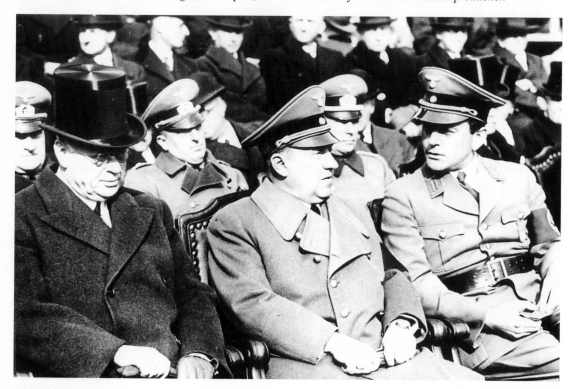

GAS CHAMBERS GAS VANS AND CREMATORIA

The first Nazi references to gassing of Jews can be found in Adolf HITLER's book, MEIN KAMPF, written in the 1920s. In it, the future German leader claimed that if 12,000 Jews had been gassed in GERMANY, "the lives of a million decent men, who would have been of value to Germany in the future, would have been saved." However, it would be many years before he could put these ideas into practice.

In September 1939, the Nazis ordered that so-called "valueless life" should be destroyed. This included the chronically ill, the handicapped and those suffering from mental disorders. The first gas chamber established for this purpose used carbon monoxide as a killing agent. Between December 1939 and August 1941, about 70,000 Germans were killed in five different "euthanasia" centers (SEE EUTHANASIA PROGRAM). Some of these centers had gas chambers, and others had disguised gas vans.

When the Germans invaded ROMANIA in June 1941, they sent in EINSATZGRUPPEN for the mass murder of the Jews. The method of killing was by shooting. The Nazis soon decided that they needed to develop a quicker and more secret means of mass

Gas van in Chelmno

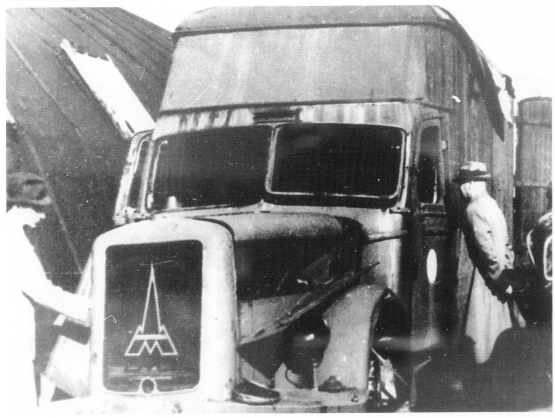

Gas chamber in Majdanek death camp

murder in order to kill all of European Jewry. Drawing upon the experience of the "euthanasia program," they decided to adapt killing by gas to the requirements of mass murder.

Crematoria in Auschwitz

In September 1941, 600 Soviet prisoners of war and 250 ill prisoners were murdered in AUSCHWITZ by using a commercial insecticide, ZYKLON B. The gas was piped into a cellar. At the same time, experiments with gas were also conducted in BUCHENWALD.

The first use of gas vans in the "FINAL SOLUTION" took place in Kalisz, POLAND, in October 1941. There, the inmates of a Jewish old age home were choked to death by exhaust fumes piped into the cabin of a truck through a specially designed tube. In December 1941, several thousand Polish Jews were also killed using gas vans in CHELMNO. The advantages of gas over shooting were clear to the Nazis: gassing could be carried out with some secrecy, and those about to be killed could be more easily fooled.

By early 1942, death by gassing (gas vans or chambers) was being carried out in DEATH CAMPS especially built by the Nazis for this purpose. In Chelmno, BELZEC, SOBIBÓR and TREBLINKA, people died by inhaling exhaust fumes from diesel engines. (Engines from captured Soviet tanks were used in Treblinka.) Gas vans quickly proved unable to handle the large number of Jews that the Nazis wished to kill.

The disposal of a vast number of bodies was also problematic. In most of the camps the victims were buried in pits. These were later opened and the remains burned (see AKTION 1005). In time, however, the Germans created crematoria, in which large numbers of bodies could be burned very quickly.

The largest center of mass murder was located at Auschwitz. At first, the gassing was carried out at the main camp. In the spring of 1942, a large satellite camp, called Birkenau or Auschwitz II, was established. The gassing was then moved to two specially adapted huts (the "white house" and the "red house") located in the birch forest surrounding Birkenau. Soon, even these proved to be too small.

Plans were drawn up, with the aid of civilian engineers, for new mass murder facilities. These were disguised as bath houses, but contained undressing rooms, gas chambers and ovens. Bodies were brought up from the underground gas chambers by means of elevators. Many German firms were eager to do the well-paid work of building and maintaining the gas chambers and crematoria, and supplying Zyklon B gas. The new facilities opened in the spring of 1943. The new crematoria could burn 4,415 bodies per day. After further experimentation,

that amount was increased to almost 8,000. Even that was not enough in 1944, and the Germans again resorted to burning bodies in pits. Thus, the facilities at Auschwitz were able to destroy up to 20,000 victims per day.

The last gassing took place at the end of October 1944, with the arrival of a transport from THERESIEN-STADT. As the Russian army advanced toward Auschwitz, the Germans hastily broke down the facilities (one of the crematoria had already been destroyed in a SONDERKOMMANDO revolt), but they did not have time to remove the rubble. After the war, many of the civilians involved in the design, construction and maintenance of the gas chambers and crematoria were charged in TRIALS OF WAR CRIMINALS. Most received light prison sentences or were acquitted.

G A S   V A N S

See GAS CHAMBERS, GAS VANS AND CREMATORIA.

GAULLE DE, CHARLES

See DE GAULLE, CHARLES.

GENERALGOUVERNEMENT

("General Government")

Name of a territorial unit with its own administration, created by the Nazis in 1939 in occupied POLAND. This area was considered to be a "racial dumping ground"—a place especially set aside by the Nazis for performing the worst aspects of their racist population policy (see RACISM). There, the Poles were subject to terrible persecution and the JEWS of Europe were put into DEATH CAMPS.

After the conquest of Poland in 1939, the General-

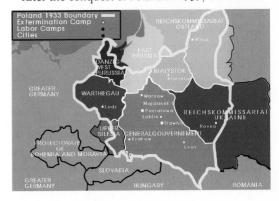

Humiliating a Jew before execution in the General-gouvernement

gouvernement was that area of Poland not annexed directly to GERMANY or given to the Soviets in the NAZI-SOVIET PACT (see map). After the German invasion of SOVIET RUSSIA in 1941, its territory was expanded, and the district of Galicia in the east became the fifth district of the Generalgouvernement. It was added to the WARSAW, Radom, LUBLIN, and KRAKÓW districts. The total population was around 16 million people, including about 2 million Jews. This number was increased by forced immigration.

Though Hans FRANK was general governor, the racial policies were in the hands of the SS and the police. They supervised the DEPORTATIONS of the Jews to the death camps of BELZEC, SOBIBÓR and TREBLINKA. The Generalgouvernement was dissolved when the Soviets overran it at the end of 1944.

GENERALPLAN OST

("General Plan East")
Scheme proposed by Nazi leaders in 1941–1942 to resettle eastern Europe with Germans, in anticipation of a German victory in WORLD WAR II.

Most discussions of the HOLOCAUST period focus on Nazi mass murders and seizures of property and lands. This gives the impression that these actions were ends unto themselves. However, as early as 1941, Heinrich HIMMLER began to set out his long-term plan for the ultimate fate of the conquered territories, to be carried out over a 25-year period following Nazi victory.

The plan called for ten million Germans to be moved into the occupied areas of POLAND, the Baltic states, BYELORUSSIA, and parts of Russia and the UKRAINE. Since 45 million people were already living in these areas, including 6 million JEWS, preparing the territory called for extermination and expulsion. As many as 31 million people were slated to be expelled to western Siberia. A complex system of "scientific" racial classification was designed by the Nazis to determine who would be expelled, exterminated or resettled.

Already in 1942, when the liquidation of Poland's Jews was at its height, German authorities made the first attempts at the implementation of the *Generalplan Ost*. Some 30,000 Germans who had been living in LITHUANIA were moved from their homes and made ready for resettlement in Poland. Between November 1942 and August 1943, Poles living in the Lublin area were forced out of their homes, which were given to Germans. As German victory became less likely, interest in the plan faded.

GENERALS' PLOT

see PLOT TO KILL HITLER.

GENOCIDE

The deliberate killing of a racial, political, religious or ethnic group. The term was first used by Raphael LEMKIN. In 1933, he submitted a proposal to the LEAGUE OF NATIONS for an international convention (agreement) on barbaric crimes and vandalism. Lemkin had a major role in writing the Genocide Convention, adopted by the United Nations on 9 December 1948. This convention was written to undercut the claims by Nazi defendants at TRIALS OF WAR CRIMINALS that they had not violated any law.

Before a mass shooting in the Sdolbunov, Soviet Union

The Genocide Convention specifically defines different aspects of the Nazi persecutions to be crimes. It prohibits: 1) the killing of persons belonging to a group (the "FINAL SOLUTION"); 2) causing serious bodily or spiritual harm to members of a group; 3) deliberately forcing a group to live under conditions that could lead to complete or partial destruction of the group (confinement to GHETTOS and starvation); 4) taking measures to prevent births among a group (STERILIZATION); and 5) forcibly taking children from a group and transferring them to another group (such as the kidnapping of Polish children and their resettlement with German families).

GENOCIDE CONVENTION

see GENOCIDE.

GENS, JACOB

(1905–1943) Head of the Jewish Police and JUDENRAT

Jacob Gens

(Jewish Council) in the VILNA GHETTO from 1942 to 1943.

When the Germans occupied Vilna on 24 June 1941, Gens was working as an accountant in the city's health department. The Nazis appointed him director of the Jewish hospital and then head of the Jewish Police. As such, Gens was forced to carry out German demands that Jews be assembled for DEPORTATION. Between September and December 1941, he was responsible for having Jews report for transport to PONARY, where they were killed. Gens personally checked people's identity cards, assuring them that they had work permits. Those without the permits—often children, the sick, and the elderly—were sent to Ponary. In Gens's own words, he was forced by the Germans to "act without conscience."

In July 1942, the Nazis appointed Gens head of the Jewish Council. Due to his tight grip over ghetto life, he was referred to by many ghetto residents as "King Jacob the First." Gens believed in "working for survival"—the idea that if Vilna Jews produced for the German economy, their lives would be spared. This proved true for a while, and the ghetto passed a period of relative calm. During this time, cultural and welfare institutions, and a medical care system opened under Gens's administration.

At first Gens cooperated with the ghetto UNDERGROUND, the United Partisan Organization (FAREYNEGTE PARTIZANER ORGANIZATSYE; FPO). However, later he declared that the FPO's smuggling of weapons into the ghetto was a danger to the entire Jewish population. The most problematic incident of Gens's career was his refusal to support FPO commander, Yitzhak WITTENBERG, which led to Wittenberg's death.

By the time the Germans liquidated the Vilna ghetto, in August and September 1943, Gens had completely lost the confidence of the ghetto population. During the September AKTIONS (killing operations), the FPO defied Gens by ordering the ghetto population not to appear for deportation. On 1 September, a clash occurred between underground members and German forces. Gens feared that this clash would cause the immediate liquidation of the ghetto. He therefore agreed to provide the Germans with a quota for FORCED LABOR in ESTONIA if the Germans would pull their forces out of the ghetto—which they did. Following these deportations, 12,000 Jews were left in the Vilna ghetto.

Gens's wife and daughter, both Lithuanians, were outside the ghetto area in Vilna. Offers were made for Gens to join his family, but he refused—despite warnings that the Germans were planning to kill him.

On 14 September 1943, Gens was summoned to GESTAPO headquarters and shot to death. The ghetto was liquidated 10 days later.

G E R M A N Y

Central European country. From 1914 to 1918, Germany had fought (together with Austria-Hungary and ITALY) World War I against the Allies (GREAT BRITAIN, FRANCE, the UNITED STATES and—until 1917—Russia). After the war, the WEIMAR REPUBLIC was established and Germany had a fully democratic government. This was, however, a period of great economic suffering and unemployment. The Allies demanded that Germany pay them massive amounts of money to compensate for their material losses in the war. The Great Depression that began in 1929 made the situation even worse. As a result, there was much unrest in Germany. Political parties and other groups arose and proposed extreme solutions to the country's problems. The Nazis were at one extreme (see NAZI PARTY) and the communists were at the other. Both won wide followings throughout the 1920s and in the early 1930s. Adolf HITLER, the head of the Nazi Party, seized power in 1933. He became the dictator of Germany, ended the Weimar Republic and democracy, and declared the THIRD REICH.

In 1933, there were over 500,000 JEWS (according to a religious definition) in Germany, which was 0.8 percent of the total population. One-third of the Jews lived in BERLIN and another third in a few other large cities. Under the Weimar Republic they had enjoyed complete legal equality. Jews had risen to high positions in politics, economics, the professions, and all areas of cultural creativity.

Immediately after the Nazis rose to power on 30 January 1933, however, they began to exclude Jews from German society. Jews rapidly lost their legal rights. They were dismissed from the civil service, denied entry to universities, and excluded from cultural life. The anti-Jewish NUREMBERG LAWS were passed in September 1935. Antisemitic actions, which had increased during the Weimar Republic, were now tolerated and even encouraged by the

Above: Nazi demonstration in Dresden, 1932

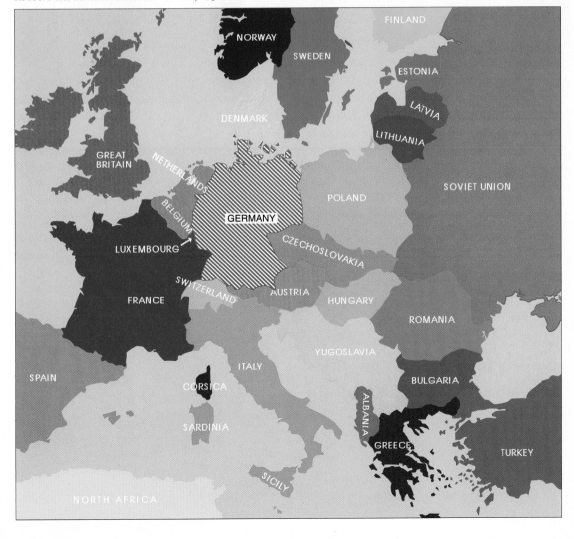

Above: *Arrest of Jewish males, 10 November 1938;*
Below: *Jews of Hamburg and Cologne deported to Lódz*

government. These came to a climax with KRISTALL-NACHT, the terrible pogrom of 9 November 1938. In those anti-Jewish riots, hundreds of synagogues were burned, Jewish homes and stores were looted and destroyed, and thousands of Jews were sent to CONCENTRATION CAMPS.

Germany's Jews organized a wide network of SELF-HELP organizations during the time of persecution and suffering. Their most important aim was to promote emigration. Some institutions were also established for relief within Germany. They included adult education centers under the leadership of the philosopher Martin Buber, publishing houses and newspapers, the KULTURBUND DEUTSCHER JUDEN, social welfare bodies (which organized theaters, orchestras, etc.), and the REICHSVERTRETUNG DER DEUTSCHEN JUDEN under Rabbi Leo BAECK and Otto HIRSCH.

In the first four years after 1933, 130,000 German Jews emigrated. With the increase in ANTISEMITISM, numbers of those leaving rose to 40,000 in 1938, and 78,000 in 1939. Another 23,000 Jews managed to leave Germany until its borders were sealed in 1941.

A decree of September 1941 forced all Jews over the age of six to wear the yellow BADGE. DEPORTATIONS of German Jews started in 1940 from Stettin to POLAND, and from Baden and the Saar region to France. From there they were sent to DEATH CAMPS. Systematic deportations from the remaining areas began in October 1941, first to LÓDZ, WARSAW, RIGA, KOVNO, and MINSK. Later, deportations went directly to AUSCHWITZ and other death camps. In May 1941, 168,972 Jews—according to the racial definitions of the Nuremberg Laws—were still registered in Germany. Their number had dropped to 14,574 by September 1944. Those remaining Jews survived because they were protected by non-Jewish spouses or had a non-Jewish parent. Approximately 200,000 German Jews died in the Nazi Holocaust.

Together with east European Jewish DISPLACED PERSONS who stayed in Germany, the small group of German Jewish survivors rebuilt Jewish communities in over 70 German cities after 1945.

GERSTEIN, KURT

(1905–1945) ss officer and head of the Waffen-SS Institute of Hygiene. An unusual character, he was a Nazi who knew about the secrets of the DEATH CAMPS,

Kurt Gerstein

and tried (unsuccessfully) to let the world know about the mass murders that were taking place there.

Gerstein was an SS member with strong Christian beliefs. He was an associate of Martin NIEMÖLLER, and had spent time in a CONCENTRATION CAMP for his beliefs. He had medical training and was therefore appointed chief disinfection officer of the Institute of Hygiene at the beginning of 1942. There he worked with ZYKLON B, the gas used to murder the Jews in the death camps. He was ordered to visit the death camps of BELZEC and TREBLINKA to recommend ways to improve the killing techniques that were being used at the newly established camps. He brought with him 100 canisters of Zyklon B gas.

After the war, Gerstein insisted that he saw the mission as a chance to find out the truth about the fate of the Jews. His accurate description of the operations of the gas chambers of Belzec is a harrowing insight into this camp.

Gerstein related his experiences to representatives of the Dutch UNDERGROUND, to Christian officials in BERLIN and to a Swedish diplomat, Baron Gören von Otter. His efforts were in vain: his reports were ignored and his written testimony had little impact at the NUREMBERG TRIAL. Arrested as a member of the SS by French forces, his despair led him to commit suicide at the end of the war.

G E S T A P O

Abridgment of Geheime Staatspolizei, Secret State Police, the German secret political police force that held wide-ranging responsibilities for shadowing, imprisoning, torturing and disposing of "opponents of Nazism." The Gestapo had already existed as a German government secret intelligence operation before the Nazis came to power. Under Nazi rule, the Gestapo became the terror of the German population and was involved in most aspects of the final solution. The Gestapo supervised the seizing of property, the deportation of Jews to concentration camps and the work of the "mobile killing units." In time, it carried out its operations completely outside of German civil law.

By 1936, the Gestapo was officially absorbed into the SS under Heinrich HIMMLER and Reinhard HEYDRICH. Even though the SS controlled the concentration camps, the Gestapo was able to send its victims to them. Once a person was arrested by the Gestapo and entered the concentration camp system, he or she was no longer protected by any existing laws in the German criminal code. Its powers to carry out the "measures necessary to their task stem from specific laws…" There was no appeal from its decisions, which the courts were not allowed to examine. Legislation passed by the Nazis allowed the Gestapo even more freedom in dealing with "political prisoners" and "enemies of the regime." In short, the Gestapo could do with its victims as it wished.

The Gestapo section headed by Adolf EICHMANN was in charge of sending the Jews from areas conquered by the Nazis to concentration camps to be murdered. Gestapo officers also headed the EINSATZGRUPPEN, killing units that operated throughout Europe. It had direct control over one camp, THERESIENSTADT, in CZECHOSLOVAKIA. By the early 1940s, the Gestapo had essentially taken control of Germany and all the conquered territories of the Reich. After the war, very few of the major figures in the Gestapo were captured and brought to trial.

An exhibition on Nazi terror is now displayed in the cellars of the former Gestapo building in Berlin

Schoolchildren in Lódz ghetto waiting in line with soup bowls

G H E T T O

Sections of cities set aside for JEWS to live in so that they would be separate from the rest of the population. The term "ghetto" comes originally from the name of the Jewish quarter in Venice, established in 1516. (In Italian the word means foundry—a place where metals are melted and cast. The Venice ghetto had been the site of a cannon foundry.) Ghettos were established in ITALY, and then in other countries in Europe, to segregate Jews.

To the Nazis, however, ghettos were more than a way of isolating Jews. They were seen as a short-term measure in the plan to destroy European Jewry through starvation, DEPORTATION, and mass murder. Most ghettos were found in Nazi-occupied eastern Europe. They were closed off by walls and barbed-wire fences. In POLAND ghettos were set up soon after the Nazis invaded in September 1939. By 1942, most of the Jews of eastern Europe were confined to over 400 ghettos. For most of Europe's Jews, the ghetto served as a last stop before being sent to their deaths.

Ghettos were extremely overcrowded and unsanitary. Many Jews died in them from disease and starvation. The largest ghetto in Poland was in WARSAW, where 450,000 Jews were crowded into an area of

1.3 square miles. It was enclosed by 11 miles of wall. Other major ghettos included LÓDZ, KRAKÓW, BIA-LYSTOK, LVOV, LUBLIN, KOVNO, VILNA, RIGA, Czestochowa, Zaglembie, and MINSK. The Nazis ordered Jews to wear special identifying BADGES and seized many Jews for FORCED LABOR. Daily life in the ghetto was governed by a Nazi-appointed Jewish Council (see JUDENRAT). The Judenrat served as both the Jews' government and as an instrument of German control. Jewish police forces were established to maintain order. They were also forced to assist with deportations. Illegal activities, such as smuggling food or weapons or joining YOUTH MOVEMENTS, were often done without the approval of the Judenrat. The Jews in the ghettos had little or no employment. They lived in filth, hunger, disease, and despair.

In some ghettos, members of the Jewish RESIS-TANCE staged armed uprisings. The largest was the WARSAW GHETTO UPRISING. Armed uprising was not the only form of resistance. Ghetto residents also worked hard to preserve their humanity by participating in cultural and religious activities. This itself was an act of defiance. Concerts and lectures were well attended. Poetry and songs were composed, sung, and recited in the ghetto.

Jews were often deported from the ghetto in a series of AKTIONEN. The first to be sent to their deaths

In Amsterdam ghetto. The sign "Juden Viertel/Joodsche Wijk" — Jewish District — was put up by the German occupiers

A main street in the Lódz ghetto

were the elderly, the sick, and the CHILDREN. By August 1944, the Nazis had completed the liquidation of Europe's Jewish ghettos. This was accomplished either by deporting all residents to DEATH CAMPS, where they were gassed, or by mass shootings by the EINSATZGRUPPEN (mobile killing units).

HUNGARY was an exception, since Jews there were not forced into ghettos until June 1944. In BUDAPEST, Jews were first placed in marked houses (Star of David houses). Then a ghetto was formally established. About 63,000 Jews without "protective passports," provided by Raoul WALLENBERG, were confined to a 0.1-square mile area. The 25,000 Jews granted "protective passports" (in the name of neutral countries) were put in an "international ghetto," and their lives were spared.

GHETTO FIGHTERS' HOUSE

(Beit Lohamei Ha-Gettaot)

Museum located at Kibbutz Lohamei Ha-Gettaot in Galilee, Northern Israel. Many of the founding members of this kibbutz were fighters in the Jewish RESISTANCE movement during WORLD WAR II. Its museum, founded in 1949, was the first museum in Israel dealing with the HOLOCAUST.

The Ghetto Fighters' House consists of two museums, a study center, a research branch, a library

Yad Layeled (children's memorial) in the Ghetto Fighters' House

and archives. All are open to the public. The main museum focuses on Jewish life in Europe before the war and all different forms of Jewish resistance during the Holocaust.

Yad la-Yeled (The Children's Memorial), opened

From the Ghetto Fighters' House permanent exhibition "Resistance and fighting back"

in 1995 and is dedicated to the 1.5 million children who perished in the Holocaust. It is an educational center for children about the life of children during the Holocaust. Its exhibits are based on authentic stories collected from diaries and TESTIMONIES. It contains three-dimensional exhibits arranged in historical order along a lane. The young visitor walking along this lane hears the stories of children who lived during the Holocaust, narrated by children of today.

Research is carried out at the museum in cooperation with the University of Haifa. The library contains 40,000 titles in various languages. The large archive collection includes original documents of the Hehalutz Youth Movement, DISPLACED PERSONS camps as well as many personal documents. There are also separate archive collections of the papers of Janusz KORCZAK and Yitzhak KATZNELSON.

GLASBERG, ALEXANDRE

(1902–1981) French priest who saved the lives of thousands of Jews during the HOLOCAUST. Born to a Jewish family in Zhitomir, Russia, Glasberg converted to Catholicism, entered the priesthood and settled in FRANCE. After the fall of France in June 1940, the country was divided into occupied and unoccupied zones. Many antisemitic laws were passed. In unoccupied VICHY France alone, some 25,000 foreign-born Jews were arrested and placed in labor brigades. To assist those Jews who were released, Glasberg founded the *Amitié Chrétienne* (Christian Friendship) under the patronage of the Catholic Church.

On 2 July 1942, the Germans ordered the Vichy government to hand over all foreign-born Jews. Glasberg promptly took the *Amitié* UNDERGROUND and continued to rescue Jews from the authorities. By December, however, with the GESTAPO close on his heels, he left the *Amitié* and joined the PARTISANS. After the war, he helped many survivors break through the British blockade and emigrate to PALESTINE.

GLIK, HIRSH

(1922–1944) Yiddish poet, songwriter, playwright, and PARTISAN fighter.

Glik was born and educated in VILNA. He showed promise as a writer at an early age. His first poems, which he wrote in his early teenage years, were written in Hebrew. They portray his involvement with the Zionist youth movement. Later, he published poetry in Yiddish-language journals.

Glik is best remembered for the songs and poems that he created after the German takeover of Vilna in June 1941. He wrote a great deal during this period, at first in the FORCED LABOR CAMP of Biala Waka. His writing in the Vilna GHETTO won prizes in two ghetto literary competitions. He also wrote in the Estonian camp of Goldfilz, to which he was deported in 1943. Glik lost his life in 1944, during an escape attempt from Goldfilz. Most of his writing did not survive the war.

Glik was an active member of the Vilna ghetto RESISTANCE movement (FAREYNEGTE PARTIZANER ORGANIZATSYE). He wrote songs to honor the accomplishments of the partisans. The song *Shtil di nakht iz oysegeshternt* ("The Quiet Night was Filled with Stars") glorifies the first successful act of sabotage carried out by the Vilna partisans against a German weapons supply train. Glik's most famous song, *Zog*

Hirsh Glik

nisht keynmol az du geyst dem letstn veg ("Never Say That You Have Reached the Final Road"), was adopted as the anthem of the Jewish resistance movement in eastern Europe. In the postwar period, this song (also known as *The Partisan Hymn*) has become part of Holocaust remembrance ceremonies throughout the world. (See box in entry on PARTISANS).

GLOBOCNIK, ODILO

(1904–1945) ss and Police official and head of AKTION (OPERATION) REINHARD, the murder of the Jews of the GENERALGOUVERNEMENT in POLAND.

Globocnik was appointed SS and Police leader for the LUBLIN district of Poland in November 1939. He was assistant to Heinrich HIMMLER, who fondly called him "Globus." Globocnik was in charge of establishing an SS power base in the Generalgouvernement, a task he carried out enthusiastically.

The DEATH CAMPS of BELZEC, SOBIBÓR, and TREBLINKA were established to murder all the Jews of the Generalgouvernement. About 2 million Jews lost their

Odilo Globocnik

lives in these camps. Globocnik requested that some of his men be rewarded with iron crosses for their "special performances."

Globocnik was also involved in the economic side of Operation Reinhard. He became executive director of Osti, an organization set up to use the FORCED LABOR of those Jews not immediately sent to the GAS CHAMBERS. Under Operation Reinhard, the money and valuables of the Polish Jews were also seized, including the gold teeth and fillings of the murdered Jews.

By 1943, there were no Jews remaining to be exploited and Globocnik was transferred to Trieste in ITALY to combat PARTISANS. He was captured by Allied troops in May 1945 and later committed suicide.

GOEBBELS, PAUL JOSEF

(1897–1945) Nazi minister of propaganda. Josef Goebbels was the son of a poor family from the Rhineland town of Rheydt. Born with a clubfoot, he was unable to serve in World War I. After Germany's defeat, he turned to radical politics and hoped to become a writer. This goal remained unfulfilled until he joined the NAZI PARTY in 1924 as the managing editor of a journal published by Gregor Strasser. That year, Goebbels met Strasser's rival, Adolf HITLER. When the feud between the two leaders came to a head, Goebbels eagerly supported Hitler.

Goebbels's reputation as a party spokesman grew rapidly. Hitler recognized his loyalty and his public speaking skills and appointed him district party leader of Berlin in 1926. There Goebbels brought the Nazi party to the national level. In 1928, he became its propaganda chief. He arranged to have Hitler flown around Germany for speaking engagements, adopted the use of blazing red posters and organized heroic funerals for party men who had been killed in brawls. He elevated HORST WESSEL to a Nazi folk hero, and launched hostile campaigns against those he blamed for Germany's problems.

Goebbels became a member of the WEIMAR parliament in 1928 and used this position to further the Nazi cause. In March 1933, he was appointed minister of popular education and culture, a ministry that reached into every aspect of German life. He was responsible for creating the many myths surrounding the THIRD REICH and its leaders, particularly the

Josef Goebbels delivers a speech to a crowd in Berlin urging Germans to boycott Jewish-owned businesses, 1933

exaltation of the "FÜHRER" concept. On 10 May 1933, he ordered the public burning of "un-German" books. He also took control of the radio, turning it into a powerful propaganda weapon. He encouraged the development of a Nazi film industry, which produced powerful propaganda films that constantly portrayed the Jews as the ultimate enemy of the Germans (see FILMS, NAZI ANTISEMITIC). In November 1938, he developed the idea of the KRISTALLNACHT pogroms.

During WORLD WAR II, Goebbels directed the Nazis' campaign of psychological warfare. He believed that the greater the lie and the more it was repeated, the greater the chance that it would be believed. He constantly stirred up prejudice against the Jews and incited other citizens to harass Jews and limit their freedom.

Goebbels's popularity with Hitler was never stable, until there was an abortive assassination attempt on Hitler in July 1944. At that time, Goebbels acted to assure Hitler's hold on power. As the Allies encircled Berlin in 1945, Goebbels remained with Hitler in his bunker under the chancellery. Hitler named Goebbels his successor, but Goebbels refused to accept. On the day after Hitler's suicide, Goebbels had his own children killed and then committed suicide with his wife. His remains were identified by Russian troops a few hours later.

GOETH, AMON LEOPOLD

(1908–1946) SS officer and commandant of the PLASZÓW CONCENTRATION CAMP.

In February and March 1942, the DEPORTATION of Jews from GHETTOS to DEATH CAMPS began in the GENERALGOUVERNEMENT region of POLAND. As an SS captain in KRAKÓW, Goeth was in charge of several of these actions, including the evacuation of the Kraków ghetto itself. At his trial after the war, he was accused of personally shooting between 30 and 90 Jews at that time. He was also charged with participating in the deportation of thousands to AUSCHWITZ and in sending Jews from the Tarnów ghetto to BELZEC. In February 1943, Goeth was given command of the Plaszów FORCED LABOR and concentration camp, which contained 10,000 inmates at its peak.

Amon Leopold Goeth

Most of these were from the Kraków ghetto and were later sent to Auschwitz. Goeth was tried before the Supreme National Tribunal of Poland, and was hanged.

GOGA, OCTAVIAN

(1881–1938) Romanian writer and poet who became a politician. Goga introduced anti-Jewish measures in ROMANIA before WORLD WAR II. In 1932, he founded the National Agrarian Party (NAP), which received financial support from the German NAZI PARTY. In 1935, the NAP merged with the National Christian League, an openly antisemitic party. Together they formed the National Christian Party. Even though that party won only 9.15 percent of the vote in the 1937 general elections, King Carol II called on Goga to form the new government. That government lasted only 44 days and was disbanded because of strong pressure from FRANCE and GREAT BRITAIN. Goga managed in that short period of time to adopt a number of measures against the Jews, including a nationality law that questioned the right of Jews to Romanian citizenship. This law led to a third of Romania's Jews being stripped of that right.

GÖRING, HERMANN

(1893–1946) Nazi leader; founder of the GESTAPO and the Luftwaffe (German air force). Born to a

Hermann Göring

wealthy family in Bavaria, GERMANY, he was sent to study in a military academy. During World War I, he served as a pilot in the air force and won many medals for bravery. However, once the war was over, he struggled to make a living and, after spending some time in Denmark, returned to Germany.

Göring became interested in the NAZI PARTY, and he got to know Adolf HITLER. Hitler offered him command of the party's private army, the SA. Göring was with Hitler during the abortive Beer Hall Putsch of 1923 in Munich. He was injured when troops turned on the Nazi demonstrators.

After spending time in Austria, Italy and Sweden, Göring returned to Germany in 1927. Since he had many connections with the nobility and with industrialists, he was sent to Berlin to secure financial support for the Nazi party. He persuaded Hitler to have him represent the Nazi party in the REICHSTAG in 1928.

> *Guns will make us powerful; butter will only make us fat (usually misquoted as "guns instead of butter").*
>
> *Hermann Göring*

Göring was appointed president of the Reichstag in 1932. As the highest-ranking Nazi in the country, he helped bring Hitler to power. When Hitler was appointed chancellor in 1933, Göring received several cabinet posts. In 1933, he became prime minister of Prussia and was one of those responsible for forming the Gestapo, which was later turned over to Heinrich HIMMLER. In 1934, he worked with Himmler to kill the SA chief Ernst RÖHM and his supporters in Hitler's frantic purge called the Night of the Long Knives. In 1935, he was appointed commander of the Luftwaffe. He was also responsible for taking Jewish property in 1937 and, for a time, was in charge of the Nazi anti-Jewish policy.

On the day WORLD WAR II broke out, Hitler appointed Göring field marshal and his heir. However, when the Luftwaffe was unable to conquer Britain and protect Germany from Allied attacks, he lost Hitler's approval and was dismissed from all his posts. He spent the final years of the war in semi-retirement on his large estate. When Germany's defeat was certain, Göring decided that Hitler had lost all power and declared himself FÜHRER. For this act, he was stripped of his rank and expelled from the Nazi party.

Göring was captured by the Allies and brought to trial at Nuremberg (see TRIALS). He did not deny responsibility for the Nazi atrocities and was sentenced to death. However, just two hours before he was to be hanged, he poisoned himself in his cell.

GOVERNMENTS-IN-EXILE

Governments of countries overrun by the Nazis that continued to operate outside their own countries. Most such governments were run in London and claimed to be the successor of the legitimate pre-war government. In addition to administrative agencies, governments-in-exile oversaw conventional military forces that fought with the Allied armies. They also controlled UNDERGROUND movements in the occupied homeland.

Communication with resistance forces at home brought every government-in-exile into direct contact with the realities of Nazi persecution, deportation, and extermination of the Jews. Almost all of them issued proclamations nullifying Nazi antisemitic laws and a few, including the Czech, Belgian and Dutch governments, encouraged (with varying degrees of success) non-Jewish civilians to rescue their fellow Jews. On the other hand, concrete rescue activities by the governments-in-exile were limited. The French National Committee never acted in behalf of French Jewry, despite the prominent membership of Jews in the government and the sympathy of its French leadership in London (and then in Algiers, after 1943). Similarly, the Polish government-in-exile made numerous sympathetic statements in behalf of the Jews, hoping thereby to gain Jewish support for their postwar political goals. However, these words were not converted into action to rescue Jews until the last minute. In fact, the Polish government-in-exile was constantly overridden by antisemitic statements by Polish troops and in the Polish exile press, creating constant scandals and much ill will.

Although useful as a means of mobilizing public opinion, the governments-in-exile hardly wielded any effective political power until after the war and, in some cases, never really at all.

GRÄBE, HERMANN

(1900–1986) German who was honored with the title "RIGHTEOUS AMONG THE NATIONS" for the aid he gave to JEWS during the HOLOCAUST. Although he was an early member of the NAZI PARTY, he consistently opposed many of its policies, particularly its ANTISEMITISM.

In 1939, Gräbe was employed in his native Solingen, GERMANY, as a construction foreman. He was transferred in October 1941 to Volhynia in UKRAINE, and given the task of establishing a new branch of the firm. He employed thousands of Jews, but in contrast to many German industrialists and businessmen who cruelly exploited FORCED LABOR, he saw to it that his workers were not abused. In November 1941, in Rovno, Gräbe prevented the massacre of many of his employees by protesting to the officer in charge. He repeated this protective action in July 1942. He secured false "Aryan" (see RACISM) papers for some of his workers (i.e., stating that they were not Jews), which allowed them to escape.

In October 1942, Gräbe witnessed a massacre of the Jews of Dubno by the EINSATZGRUPPEN. His moving testimony about this (and about the earlier attempted Rovno massacre) was often quoted at the

Hermann Gräbe (left) receiving the medal for the "Righteous among the Nations" at Yad Vashem, 1966

NUREMBERG TRIAL. As a result of this publicity, Gräbe was rejected in Germany, and he moved to the United States. In 1966, he planted a tree on the Avenue of the Righteous at YAD VASHEM in Jerusalem.

GREAT BRITAIN

Country in northwest Europe. The JEWS of Britain showed deep concern for the suffering of their brothers in Europe during the HOLOCAUST period. However, British governments, except for a few leaders, showed little practical sympathy for the persecuted Jews.

Refugees from GERMANY—not all of them Jewish—began arriving in Great Britain in 1933. The British public was moved by the events of the 1938 KRISTALL-NACHT pogroms, after which the government was more generous in opening its doors to Jewish child

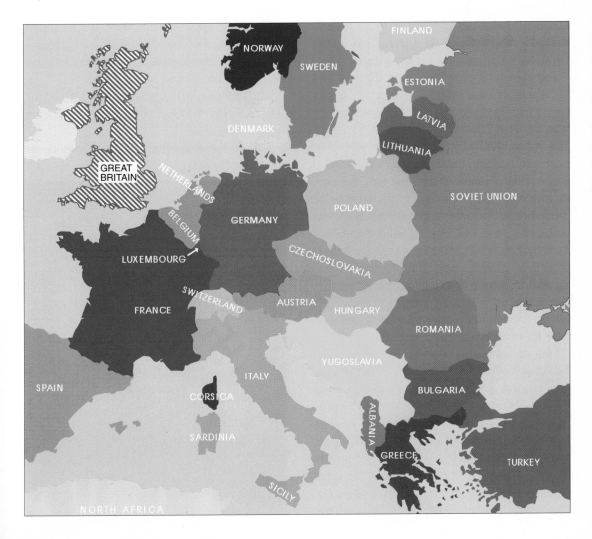

Downed German aircraft in London

refugees. By the time WORLD WAR II closed the borders of Europe the following year, 73,000 refugees had been admitted. The Jewish community played its part in fund-raising and in helping the newcomers. British Jews guaranteed that these refugees would not be a burden on the country. That promise persuaded the government to let in so many.

The main disagreement between the Jews and the government was over the question of PALESTINE. After World War I, the British had been granted the mandate over Palestine by the LEAGUE OF NATIONS. This meant that they ruled Palestine. They had promised the Jews that the land would become a Jewish National Home. At the same time, however, they were very sensitive to strong opposition by the Arabs to Jewish settlement in Palestine. In the period leading up to World War II, and during the war itself, the British felt the need to please the Arabs in order to have their support. The price paid for Arab support for Britain was to limit immigration to Palestine severely (see WHITE PAPER OF 1939). If the gates of Palestine had been open to Jews at that time, many Jews from Europe could have been saved.

London, was the focus of intensive Jewish and Zionist diplomatic activity, trying both to get more Jews into Palestine and to form a JEWISH BRIGADE in the Allied armies. British Prime Minister Winston CHURCHILL sympathized with the Jews and Zionism. However, he insisted that his first task was to defeat Adolf HITLER—only after that was done could he consider the question of Palestine. Meanwhile, other members of the government and the Civil Service opposed the Jewish requests. The official policy was

not to let any more refugees into Britain, and not to let large numbers of refugees into other parts of the British Empire (including Palestine).

In the summer of 1940, panic swept Britain after the fall of so many west European countries. The British were particularly alarmed at what had happened in NORWAY. There, local traitors had collaborated with the Nazi invaders. Fearing a German invasion themselves, the British imprisoned "enemy aliens," that is non-British nationals, including the refugees. Several thousand were deported to CANADA and AUSTRALIA (some of these lost their lives when their boats were torpedoed). Others were imprisoned in camps in Britain, particularly in the Isle of Man in the Irish Sea. Gradually, as the threat of invasion passed, they were released. Many of the men served in the Pioneer Corps of the British army. After the war, some of the Jewish refugees moved on to other parts of the British Empire and the United States. Those who remained became British citizens and were absorbed into the nation. A considerable number of refugees, especially scientists, made important contributions to the war effort.

When the news of the "FINAL SOLUTION" reached the world, the British House of Commons stood for a

Exhibit in Beth Shalom Holocaust Education Center near Nottingham, England

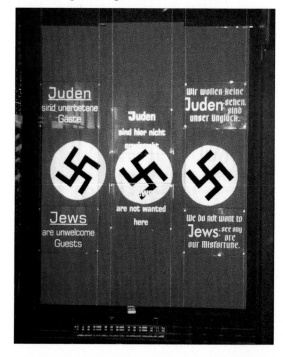

moment of silence in tribute to the victims (December 1942). However, this had almost no practical follow-up. The request that the British air force bomb the railroad leading to AUSCHWITZ was rejected on military grounds (see AUSCHWITZ BOMBING). The British took strong measures to prevent immigrants without permits from reaching Palestine. Those caught were deported to distant parts of Africa.

The liberation of the BERGEN-BELSEN concentration camp by British troops, in 1945, sent a wave of horror across Britain. Nevertheless, the British still kept their own gates closed to immigration and those of Palestine. Only because Palestine's Jews revolted against the British did Britain give up its mandate over Palestine. In 1948, the State of ISRAEL was established there, providing a home for the Holocaust survivors.

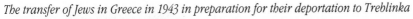

G R E E C E

Country in southeast Europe. When the Italians attacked Greece in 1940–1941, 13,000 Jews were serving in the Greek army—613 of them were killed and 3,750 were wounded. The Greeks were able to hold off the Italians, but when the Germans joined the struggle in April 1941, all of Greece soon came under Axis control. Greece was divided between the Axis countries into three areas: GERMANY controlled Crete, Macedonia and eastern Thrace (including SALONIKA); BULGARIA annexed most of Thrace; and ITALY took the rest of the mainland and islands. This brought 55,000 Jews into the hands of the Germans, 13,000 into the hands of the Italians and 5,000 to 6,000 into the hands of the Bulgarians.

At first, the Germans delayed their attack on the Jews of Greece. One reason was that the Italians did not want to discriminate against the JEWS. This prevented the Nazis from separating the Jews from the rest of the population. Jews in the German section recognized this difference, and many escaped into Italian-occupied Greece. The Germans tried to halt this outflow by demanding that Jews wear the yellow BADGE. The Italians refused to require the badge.

The systematic destruction of Greek Jewry, which began in early 1943, had three separate phases. The Jews of Salonika in German-occupied Greece were the first to be forced into GHETTOS for DEPORTATION. They were soon followed by the Jews in Bulgarian Thrace.

The Italians repeatedly refused to deport the 13,000 Jews living in their Greek territories, even though the Germans pressured them. The Italians

The transfer of Jews in Greece in 1943 in preparation for their deportation to Treblinka

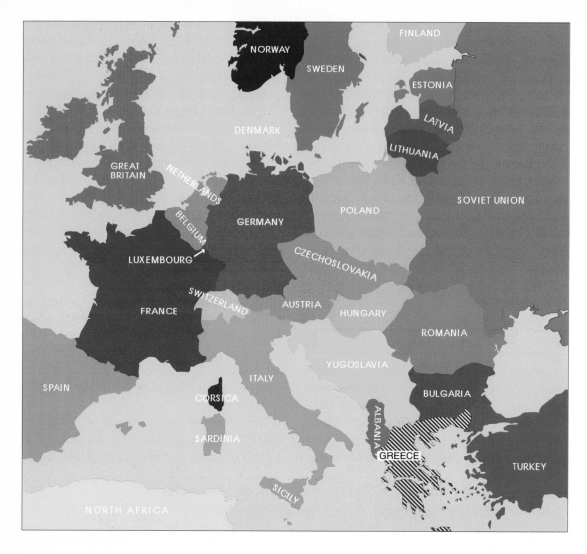

knew what the Germans planned for the Jews. On a number of occasions, the Italians announced that Jews in their territories would be brought into Italy proper, or could be concentrated together on the Greek islands. However, after Italy broke away from the Axis in September 1943, Germany seized all of Italian Greece. Thirteen thousand Jews lost their Italian protectors.

Athens' Chief Rabbi Ilia Barzilai recognized the danger of German occupation. In September 1943, he escaped to a nearby village disguised as a peasant. From there, he called upon his people to hide or join partisan groups. His call was echoed by Archbishop Theophilus Damaskinos of Athens, who encouraged Orthodox Christians to shelter Jews. These calls to action saved the lives of many Jews. Rabbi Barzilai, for example, later arranged for 600

Jews to be smuggled by partisans to neutral Turkey in exchange for money and supplies provided by Jews in PALESTINE.

Dieter WISLICENY and Alois BRUNNER directed the anti-Jewish actions in Greece on behalf of Adolf EICHMANN. In October 1943, the full range of Nazi ANTI-JEWISH LAWS was extended across the newly occupied territories. Jews were ordered to register themselves and their property—or be shot.

In March 1944, 800 Jews living in Athens were rounded up and deported by the WEHRMACHT and Greek police. They were sent to the DEATH CAMPS in POLAND. The property of these Jews was distributed to the general population in order to improve relations between the occupiers and the occupied. Many other Jews—perhaps 2,000—had been hidden due to the activism of Rabbi Barzilai and Christian

Greeks. Many Jews in smaller towns and on the islands also avoided deportation as the warnings of Rabbi Barzilai and Archbishop Damaskinos echoed across the country. On the island of Volos, for example, 752 Jews were hidden and 130 deported. However, 1,800 to 2,000 Jews from Corfu were deported to their deaths in June 1944, as were 1,700 to 2,200 Jews from Rhodes one month later.

A number of Greek Jews participated in the uprising in AUSCHWITZ-Birkenau in October 1944. Others were among the inmates who blew up a crematorium at the death camp.

Of Greece's prewar Jewish population of some 77,000, between 60,000 to 67,000 died in the Holocaust. Fewer than 2,000 Jews returned from the camps.

GROSS-ROSEN

Nazi CONCENTRATION CAMP located south of the town of Gross-Rosen (Rogoznica) in Lower SILESIA (POLAND). The Gross-Rosen complex was set up as a satellite camp of SACHSENHAUSEN in the summer of 1940. It was originally built as a work camp, and initially housed fewer than 100 prisoners. They were employed as FORCED LABORERS in the construction of the camp and at the nearby granite quarry. As the German armaments industry grew in the occupied eastern territories, Gross-Rosen increased in size and number of prisoners. It became an independent concentration camp in May 1941.

Before its evacuation in February 1945, the Gross-Rosen complex had expanded to include munitions factories and a network of 70 satellite camps, with a prisoner population of 80,000. The main camp held at least 10,000 people of nearly every European nationality. Over one-third of the prisoners were female. In the last years of its existence, Jewish prisoners were the largest group of Gross-Rosen inmates. Beginning in late 1943, some 60,000 Jews were sent there, mostly from Poland and HUNGARY, to serve as forced laborers.

Working and living conditions at Gross-Rosen were extremely harsh. The camp earned a grim reputation for its unusually high death rate. The grueling labor, unsanitary conditions, poor food, and brutal treatment by the guards all contributed to the high death toll. Of the estimated 120,000 prisoners who passed through Gross-Rosen and its subcamps, 40,000 died.

As Soviet forces approached in January 1945, the Germans began to evacuate the Gross-Rosen complex. In early February, the inmates of the main camp were sent to concentration camps deeper within the borders of the Reich. Forty thousand prisoners—half of them Jews—were forced on DEATH MARCHES to other concentration camps.

GRÜNINGER, PAUL

(1891–1972) Swiss police commandant at St. Gallen on the Austrian border during WORLD WAR II; one of the "RIGHTEOUS AMONG THE NATIONS."

On 19 August 1938, SWITZERLAND closed its borders to Jews fleeing from the Nazis. However, Grüninger permitted thousands of Jews to enter the country. He falsified entry documents by dating them back to before the border was closed. In this manner he saved over 3,000 people.

Grüninger was tried for fraud by the Swiss authorities and dismissed from his post. He lost his pension. He died a poor and broken man at the age of 82. In 1971, he was recognized by YAD VASHEM as a "Righteous among the Nations" and in 1977, five

Paul Grüninger (left)

years after his death, he was forgiven by the state as a result of media attention praising his deeds. In November 1995, the St. Gallen court retried his case posthumously and gave him a full pardon.

GRYNSZPAN, HERSCHEL

(1921–?) The assassin of a German diplomat. Grynszpan was born into a Polish-Jewish family living in Hanover, GERMANY. In 1938 he moved to Paris, FRANCE. Soon after that, he became infuriated to learn that his family, together with other Polish JEWS living in Germany, was being deported to POLAND. Grynszpan decided to assassinate an important German official in order to draw attention to those Jews. When he presented himself at the German embassy in Paris, he was introduced to Ernst vom Rath, one of the senior diplomats. Grynszpan suddenly drew his pistol and mortally wounded him. After the shooting, he immediately gave himself up to the police.

Vom Rath died two days later. The Germans used his death as an excuse to organize a massive assault on German Jewry: KRISTALLNACHT. The outbreak of the war interfered with plans to put Grynszpan on trial in France. After the German conquest of France, Grynszpan was turned over to the Germans. A great show trial was planned by the German propaganda minister Joseph GOEBBELS, but this never took place. The final fate of Grynszpan remains a mystery, but it is unlikely that he was alive at the war's end.

GUNSKIRSCHEN

see MAUTHAUSEN.

GURS CAMP

Internment (prison) camp in southern FRANCE.

Gurs was one of the first and largest CAMPS established in prewar France. It was located in the Pyrenee Mountains of southwestern France, about 50 miles from the Spanish border.

Gurs was established by the French government in spring 1939. Its main purpose was to house Spanish republican refugees fleeing SPAIN after the Spanish Civil War.

After the division of France in June 1940, Gurs was located in the unoccupied zone under the juris-

Herschel Gryszpan (covering face) arrested after his attack on Ernst vom Rath in the German embassy in Paris

diction of the VICHY government. At this time, many REFUGEES flooded into the unoccupied zone. Most were Jews fleeing from the invading German army in western Europe. Many were interned in Gurs and other camps in the area. Thousands of Jews expelled from the Baden and Palatinate regions of GERMANY were also interned in Gurs. Some of these were freed over the next two years and escaped from Europe. The prisoners at Gurs suffered from poor sanitation and a shortage of food and water. Over a thousand died from disease.

In November 1942, the southern zone of France was occupied by the Germans. DEPORTATIONS of Jews and other refugees from internment camps in the south began. They were first deported to DRANCY, a transit camp outside PARIS, then to DEATH CAMPS in occupied POLAND. Between August 1942 and November 1943, about 6,000 JEWS were deported from Gurs to Drancy.

Allied forces liberated Gurs in the summer of 1944.

GUSEN CAMP

see MAUTHAUSEN.

A sewing workshop for women in Gurs camp, France

G Y P S I E S

A nomadic people originating in India who reached Europe in the 15th century. Like other groups seen by the Nazis as inferior, they were singled out for persecution, deportation and murder. Of an esti-

A group of Gypsy prisoners, awaiting instructions from their German captors, in the Belzec camp

Deportation of Gypsies from Austria

mated 936,000 Gypsies in Nazi-occupied territories, it is believed that about 220,000 were murdered.

In 1937, Heinrich HIMMLER ordered the Reich Center for Fighting the Gypsy Menace to draft racial definitions for Gypsies. The Nazis felt that the real threat was the possibility of a mixture of Gypsy and German blood. Ninety percent of the Gypsies living within GERMANY were categorized as MISCHLINGE, or mixed-race Gypsies. It was intended that eventually they were to be deported or killed. Others who were considered "socially adapted" were sterilized. However, Himmler found the other 10 percent, especially members of the Sinti and Lalleri tribes, to be of particular interest because they were of "pure" racial type. Rudolf HÖSS, the commandant of AUSCHWITZ, in his testimony after the war said: "Himmler wanted to preserve these two main Gypsy stocks. In his view they were the direct descendants of the original Indo-Germanic race and had preserved their ways and customs more or less pure and intact."

Throughout Nazi-occupied Europe during WORLD WAR II, Gypsies were interned, then deported to slave labor and death camps. Tens of thousands were killed by the EINSATZGRUPPEN and their collabora-

tors in Eastern Europe. A Gypsy family camp was created at Auschwitz-Birkenau, where 19,000 were killed. Gypsy children, especially twins and those with physical handicaps, were subjected to cruel MEDICAL EXPERIMENTS conducted by Josef MENGELE. On 31 July 1944, the Gypsy camp at Auschwitz was brought to an end as all its men, women and children were sent to the GAS CHAMBERS. Thousands of Gypsies were also deported to the camps at BERGEN-BELSEN, BUCHENWALD, DACHAU, MAUTHAUSEN and RAVENSBRÜCK. Five thousand Gypsies were interned in the LÓDZ ghetto and from there moved to the CHELMNO death camp, where they were gassed in mobile killing vans. However, the action against the Gypsies was not pursued in many places as vindictively and aggressively as that against the Jews. ROMANIA and HUNGARY, for example, both had large Gypsy populations. Although many were sent to their deaths, considerable numbers were spared.

Gypsies who had lived in the same place for two years were not killed. It was the nomadic Gypsies who were regarded as asocials and were murdered. Unlike the Jews, the criterion was connected more to life-style than to racial type and the policy of extermination was selective rather than absolute.

b

HAAVARA ("Transfer") AGREEMENT

Zionist rescue effort, based on a clearing agreement in the 1930s between the German Zionist Federation and the Nazi regime. This deal granted permission for German JEWS planning to emigrate to PALESTINE to transfer a portion of their assets to Palestine.

The agreement was formally accepted in August 1933. Before leaving, the emigrant placed his or her money in a German bank. Once in Palestine, he or she would be reimbursed in goods or be given money for the deposit.

By 1935, only 2,700 German Jews had moved to Palestine under Haavara. Then the JEWISH AGENCY began to supervise the agreement, working to increase the number of participants.

Those opposed to the deal called it an "agreement with the devil," since it helped support the Nazis financially. Those in favor of the deal did not argue that it was good—only that it was necessary. They believed there was no other way to rescue German Jews along with their possessions.

As the situation in GERMANY worsened in 1938 and 1939, Haavara became the only practical means for Jewish emigration on a large scale. For that reason alone, the Zionists wanted to continue the deal. They negotiated similar agreements with eastern European countries until the outbreak of WORLD WAR II in September 1939, when Haavara became impossible to continue. It has been estimated that between 20,000 and 50,000 Jews entered Palestine as a result of the Haavara agreement.

HAMBURG

GERMANY's largest port city and a major German cultural, economic, and shipping center.

The Jewish community in Hamburg was Germany's fourth largest. It numbered 16,885 in 1933.

Hamburg Jews had very high levels of assimilation and intermarriage with non-Jews. Between 1933 and 1937, as Nazi persecution grew, over 5,000 Hamburg Jews left Germany. More followed after the KRISTALLNACHT pogroms of November 1938.

Although many Hamburg residents opposed the violence and destruction of Kristallnacht, they did little to help the Jews.

DEPORTATIONS of Hamburg Jews began in 1941, when 3,148 Jews were deported to RIGA, LÓDZ and MINSK. During 1942, some 1,800 Jews were sent to AUSCHWITZ and THERESIENSTADT. In all, nearly 8,000 Hamburg Jews died during the Holocaust.

At the Neuengamme CONCENTRATION CAMP, near Hamburg, 50,000 Jewish and non-Jewish prisoners lost their lives. Hamburg was liberated in April 1945 by British soldiers. The soldiers helped to restore the few hundred surviving Jews back to health.

HASSELL, ULRICH VON

(1881–1944) German diplomat involved in the anti-Nazi resistance. Hassell was sympathetic at first to the goals of Nazism, even though he considered most Nazis to be vulgar. When he was ambassador to ITALY, he opposed the Rome-Berlin Axis, since he believed that it would bring GERMANY into conflict with GREAT BRITAIN. He was dismissed from his post as ambassador to Italy in 1938, but he continued to lecture on economics throughout Europe.

He was also a member of the Wednesday Club, a small group of German intellectuals that met regularly to discuss science and the arts. The group became one of the main opposition movements in Germany.

Members of the Wednesday Club came from three key parts of German society in which there was opposition to Adolf HITLER: the diplomatic corps, the army, and the civilian administration. They tried to convince leading generals to over-throw Hitler in a coup d'état (the sudden over-throw of a government), and to make a peace treaty with Britain. Hassell believed that Germany could still keep the land it had conquered under a new government. He wanted to set up Wednesday Club member Carl Goerdeler (the mayor of Leipzig) as prime minister and himself as foreign minister. The generals, however, hesitated to cooperate. Hassell was soon being watched by the GESTAPO. After the coup attempt of 1944 (see PLOT TO KILL HITLER) he was arrested and hanged. His diaries, which were hidden in a tea chest in his home, were found after the war. They became a major source of information about German resistance to Hitler.

HAUTVAL, ADELAIDE

(1906–) French physician and "RIGHTEOUS AMONG THE NATIONS."

While traveling to her mother's funeral in April 1942, Dr. Hautval was arrested for illegally crossing from VICHY FRANCE into the unoccupied zone of France. When she was in jail awaiting trial, she protested the mistreatment of the Jewish prisoners. She was then branded a "friend of the Jews," forced to wear a yellow BADGE, and sent to AUSCHWITZ. She

was put to work there as a doctor, and protected the inmates. On one occasion, when a typhus epidemic broke out, she was able to keep the epidemic a secret. This saved the lives of infected women who would have been sent directly to the GAS CHAMBERS. She refused to cooperate when she was ordered by the chief SS doctors at Auschwitz to assist in MEDICAL EXPERIMENTS on the inmates. In 1965, she was honored by YAD VASHEM as a "Righteous among the Nations."

HE-HALUTZ HA-LOHEM

see PIONEER FIGHTERS.

HEIL HITLER

The Nazi salute, meaning "Hail Hitler" (based on the ancient salutation to Roman emperors). The raised-arm greeting came from the Italian fascists; "Heil" is a royal greeting. The Nazi salute was first used publicly by crowds who saluted Adolf HITLER upon his release from prison in April 1924. Josef GOEBBELS made it the regular greeting between NAZI PARTY members even in Hitler's absence. The custom was to raise the arm and say "Heil, mein

German citizens saluting Adolf Hitler at the 11th Olympic Games, Berlin 1936

Führer" (Hail, my leader), when addressing Hitler directly.

HERRENVOLK

German for "master race." This concept, adopted by the Nazis, held that ARYANS, or Germans were members of a super-race. The basis for this idea can be traced back to French and German philosophers. They said that each nation has its own special preferences, language, history and destiny. In the 19th century, the French author Joseph-Arthur de Gobineau wrote his "Essay on the Inequality of Human Races." In it he argued that Aryans are superior and that this should be expressed in the political arena. This idea became very important in GERMANY where the Nazis saw themselves as a master race with other races—such as Slavs—destined to be inferior. The Jewish "race" was to be wiped out.

HESS, RUDOLF

(1894–1987) Nazi leader. He took part in the failed Munich coup of 1923, when Adolf HITLER tried to take over the Bavarian government. He was jailed with Hitler and during this time wrote down from dictation and edited much of Hitler's book, MEIN KAMPF. Following the Nazi rise to power in January 1933, Hess was appointed Hitler's deputy as leader of the NAZI PARTY. He later served as a minister in Hitler's cabinet.

Hess is best known for an unusual mission undertaken in May 1941. He flew to England, where he tried to convince the British that peace was possible with GERMANY. He was arrested and held in England until the conclusion of the war. Upon hearing of Hess's mission, Hitler condemned it as the act of a lunatic.

Following the war, Hess was tried at the Nuremberg TRIALS. He was convicted of crimes against peace and sentenced to life imprisonment. He served his sentence in isolation at Spandau Prison, West Germany, until he committed suicide in 1987.

HEYDRICH, REINHARD

(1904–1942) Nazi ss leader who was a central planner and executor of the "FINAL SOLUTION." Heydrich joined the SS in 1931 as chief of its Security Service (the SD, or Sicherheitsdienst) after being dishonorably discharged from the German navy in that same year. Working closely with SS chief Heinrich

Rudolf Hess seated in airplane, on the right, 1934

Reinhard Heydrich

HIMMLER, Heydrich used policies of ruthlessness and blackmail to take over the GESTAPO in 1936.

By 1938 Heydrich controlled many of the Nazi anti-Jewish policies, and he strongly emphasized "forced emigration" for the Jews. He served as a key planner of the KRISTALLNACHT pogroms of November 1938, including the arrests of thousands of Jews at that time. After the war broke out in 1939, Heydrich ordered the EINSATZGRUPPEN to force Polish Jewry into GHETTOS. Jews from the annexed areas of POLAND, GERMANY and AUSTRIA were deported to larger towns in order to be near railroads in preparation for an undisclosed "final aim" which Heydrich mentioned in his orders.

As the Nazis prepared to invade the SOVIET UNION in 1941, Heydrich ordered *Einsatzkommando* units to carry out the immediate murder of a million Soviet Jews and officials. Shortly after, Heydrich called together the infamous WANNSEE CONFERENCE, which met on 20 January 1942, to plan the "Final Solution": the mass murder of the Jews of Europe.

In 1941, Heydrich was appointed governor of Bohemia and Moravia. He was killed by Czech resistance fighters in 1942. In response, Nazi troops killed all the men in the Czech village of LIDICE, and burned the town to the ground. AKTION REINHARD, the operation for the extermination of Polish Jewry, was named for him.

H I C E M

American agency for assisting emigrants formed in 1927. Its name came from the initials of the three founding organizations that funded its activities: the New York based HIAS (Hebrew Immigrant Aid Society), the ICA (Jewish Colonization Association), which worked during wartime mostly in South America, and the Emig-Direkt (a Berlin-based organization dealing with Jewish migration), which operated from GERMANY but had to withdraw in 1934. Beginning in 1940, Hicem worked largely through the AMERICAN JEWISH JOINT DISTRIBUTION COMMITTEE (JDC). By September 1939, it had bureaus in 32 countries throughout Europe, the Far East and South and Central America. Their purpose was to advise and prepare REFUGEES for emigration and to provide practical help at points of departure and arrival.

After June 1940, Hicem moved its headquarters from PARIS to Lisbon in PORTUGAL. By July 1940, Lisbon had become the main avenue of escape from Nazi Europe, since it was a neutral port. During its first two years, Hicem helped large numbers of refugees to emigrate via Lisbon—some 25,000 in 1940, and 15,000 in 1941. After 1941, the numbers of refugees able to reach Portugal dropped, but in total some 90,000 had used this route by the end of the war.

Hicem worked with the JDC and other aid organizations to help refugees depart from Lisbon aboard neutral Portuguese ships. The JDC was in charge of arranging financial matters, such as booking tickets for passengers on available ships. Hicem took care of the practical aspects of refugee aid: giving out tickets and providing advice about visas and other matters.

Hicem's bureaus in South and Central America, the Caribbean and SHANGHAI continued to help refugees with resettlement throughout the HOLOCAUST period.

During 1944 and 1945, as the Germans retreated, offices were reopened in Europe. In October 1945, the organization was closed and HIAS took over its work.

HILFSVEREIN DER DEUTSCHEN JUDEN

("Relief Organization of German Jews")
German Jewish organization established in 1901 to assist Jewish communities in other countries in need. It helped to create Jewish educational and social welfare institutions in eastern Europe and the Middle East before the outbreak of World War I.

During the period of the WEIMAR REPUBLIC (1918–1933), the organization's activities centered mostly on organizing Jewish emigration from eastern Europe through GERMANY to destinations overseas.

After 1933, the Hilfsverein was forced to concentrate on relief efforts among German Jews. Although at first it called upon German JEWS to remain in Germany, it helped over 90,000 people who decided to emigrate to countries other than PALESTINE. (Those who left for Palestine were assisted by the JEWISH AGENCY.)

After the NUREMBERG LAWS of September 1935, the Hilfsverein developed a four-year plan of organized emigration from Germany. However, the increase in antisemitic actions and the growing need for emergency relief made it difficult to stick to an emigration plan. In 1939, the Hilfsverein was officially dissolved, but it continued to exist until 1941 as an emigration section of the REICHSVERTRETUNG DER DEUTSCHEN JUDEN.

HIMMLER, HEINRICH

(1900–1945) Head of the SS (*Reichsführer*-SS), major architect of the "FINAL SOLUTION" and one of HITLER's main advisors.

Himmler was active in the NAZI PARTY from the mid-1920s. He served the party by collecting information about its supposed enemies, specifically Jews and communists. In 1925, he was appointed deputy leader of the SS; four years later, he became its head. At that time, the SS was a small organization that served as Adolf Hitler's bodyguards. Himmler transformed the organization into a powerful, elite army that would later run the entire CONCENTRATION CAMP and DEATH CAMP systems.

Inspired by racist ideology, he worked to turn the SS into a racially superior organization. All members of the SS were required to have pure Aryan ancestry, Nordic physical characteristics, marry women of pure Aryan ancestry and be committed to having at least four children. Himmler believed that he could create within the SS a foundation for a master race of Aryans who would then rule the world.

When Hitler came to power in 1933, Himmler became the commander of the political police. That same year, Himmler established DACHAU, the first concentration camp. During the 1930s he was able to destroy the SA, an organization that challenged the power of the SS.

In the late 1930s and early 1940s, Himmler became increasingly powerful in Nazi GERMANY. In 1938, he was central in organizing the KRISTALLNACHT pogroms, during which synagogues were burned down and Jewish stores and businesses were vandalized and looted. JEWS were beaten and many were taken to Dachau. In 1939, when POLAND was invaded, Himmler was given control of that territory. In 1943, he was appointed Minister of the Interior and was in charge of all propaganda, intelligence, the police force, the courts and the civil service system.

As he became more and more powerful, Himmler was able to put his theories of racial purity into practice. He fully believed that the Aryans were the superior race, which was being contaminated by "inferior" races, particularly the Jews. He believed that by exterminating Jews and other "sub-humans"

Heinrich Himmler (foreground, center) and his entourage visiting a prisoner-of-war camp while on a tour of the eastern Front in 1941

he was doing a great service to Germany and to the world. This idea was the basis for the "FINAL SOLUTION," the plan to murder millions of Jews. To carry this out he used the SS to develop and run the entire concentration and death camp system. He oversaw the gassing and murder of millions of people and became one of the worst murderers in history. After 1943, Himmler also supervised the mass extermination of Slavs and Russians in the east.

In 1945, Himmler realized that Germany was not going to win WORLD WAR II. He secretly attempted to negotiate with the Allies in order to continue the war in the east. Hitler found out about his secret negotiations with the Western powers and expelled him from the Nazi Party. When the war ended, Himmler tried to escape Germany disguised as a soldier, but was arrested by British troops. On 23 May 1945, he committed suicide by swallowing poison.

HINDENBURG, PAUL VON

(1847–1934) German soldier and president of GERMANY who appointed Adolf HITLER as chancellor in 1933.

Hindenburg was born into the lower Prussian nobility. He was a career army officer who rose to the

President Paul von Hindenburg (right) with Adolf Hitler, March 12, 1933

post of field marshal of the German army during World War I. He was regarded as a national hero. After the war, he helped to spread the "legend of a stab in the back." According to this idea, Germany was defeated by its internal enemies rather than on the battleground. Following the death of Friedrich Ebert, the first president of WEIMAR Germany, Hindenburg was elected president in 1925. Hindenburg represented the conservative forces in Germany. Although he personally favored the ways of pre-democratic Germany, as president he defended the Weimar Republic against its enemies.

In 1932, the 85-year old Hindenburg was re-elected. This time, he was supported by the center parties and the social democrats. He ran against the rightist parties who presented Adolf Hitler as their candidate, and received a third of the votes. Between 1930 and 1933, the German parliament was blocked by a majority of extremist parties without any clear majority. Hindenburg became active in appointing and dismissing various governments. After hesitating at first, he appointed Hitler as chancellor on 30 January 1933. Hindenburg remained president, with merely ceremonial duties, until his death on 2 August 1934.

HIRSCH, OTTO

(1885–1941) German Jewish leader. Hirsch was prominent in Jewish affairs from the 1920s. He became the chairman of the REICHSVERTRETUNG DER DEUTSCHEN JUDEN, the national organization of German Jewry, when it was established in 1933 following the rise of the Nazis. Hirsch devoted the rest of his life to defending his people and working for their welfare. He was arrested for the first time in 1935 for standing up to German authorities. He continued his efforts after his release. He was arrested once more in 1938 following KRISTALLNACHT, and was sent to the SACHSENHAUSEN concentration camp, where he remained for two weeks. When he was released, he tried desperately to find avenues of escape for German JEWS. He traveled to western Europe and the United States to try to set up refugee camps. Although he could have remained safe in those countries, he always returned to continue his work. Following the DEPORTATION of Jews from the German province of Baden in October

1940, Hirsch strongly protested to the German authorities. His organization proclaimed a day of fasting for all Jews in Germany. He was arrested a third time on 16 February 1941, and sent to the MAUTHAUSEN concentration camp, where he was tortured to death.

HIRSCHMANN, IRA ARTHUR

(1901–1989) American Jewish rescue worker during the HOLOCAUST, prominent businessman and vice president of Bloomingdale's department store in New York from 1938 to 1946. In 1938, Hirschmann served as a member of the U.S. delegation to the EVIAN CONFERENCE and in February 1944, he was sent by the WAR REFUGEE BOARD to facilitate the rescue of Jews from ROMANIA, BULGARIA and HUNGARY via Turkey, which was a neutral country during the war. In March 1944, Hirschmann, with the help of the International RED CROSS in Romania, managed to bring 48,000 Jews back from TRANSNISTRIA, to Romania.

Other rescue attempts that Hirschmann initiated were full of obstacles, but he succeeded in arranging the escape routes via the Black Sea to Turkey, and via the Aegean Sea from GREECE to Turkey. Most of the Jewish refugees who survived these escapes were taken to PALESTINE. Hirschmann's pressure on the Bulgarian government helped to end the persecution of Bulgarian Jewry and to regain full rights for the 45,000 Jews of Bulgaria.

In 1946, Hirschmann was appointed special inspector for the UNITED NATIONS RELIEF AND REHABILITATION ADMINISTRATION.

HISTORIOGRAPHY OF THE HOLOCAUST

The study of all aspects of the history of the Holocaust. During the Holocaust itself, efforts were made to collect and hide documents about the tragedy. Before meeting his death in the RIGA GHETTO, the famous historian Simon Dubnow exclaimed, "Jews! Record Everything!" The best known of these efforts was the Oneg Shabbat group inside the WARSAW ghetto. Under the direction of the historian Emanuel RINGELBLUM, it assembled a wealth of documentation on conditions in the ghetto and hid it in milk cans buried under ground. Ringelblum

and his assistants did not survive the war. However, all but one of the cans were dug up after the war. Their contents provided much of what is known about life in the Warsaw ghetto. Even in DEATH CAMPS efforts were made to record events for future generations.

Immediately after the war, a number of organizations were created in order to collect data about the Nazi crimes. The aim of much of this effort was to collect evidence for use at the war crimes TRIALS held in Nuremberg and elsewhere. Although some survivors published memoirs, the great majority chose to remain silent. Thus, much of the information included in the first history books on the Holocaust came from captured German documents. Personal TESTIMONIES played a secondary role.

The first attempts at writing a general history were those of the French historian Léon Poliakov, who published his *Breviare de la haine* in 1951. In 1953, Gerald Reitlinger published *The Final Solution—The Attempt to Exterminate the Jews of Europe*. Other important general works which came out during this period were those of Joseph Tenenbaum (*Race and Reich* and *Underground*) and Philip Friedman, who assembled a detailed bibliography.

In 1960, Raul Hilberg published *The Destruction of the European Jews*. As the author explained, this is not a book about the Jews, but about the people who destroyed the Jews. It remains one of the most thorough treatments of the subject. The book received considerable criticism, since it depicts the Jews as passive and even indifferent to their fate. Some charged Hilberg with relying too heavily on captured German documents, which paint a negative view of the Jews.

The EICHMANN trial in Israel, in the early 1960s, awakened considerable interest in the Holocaust, both in Israel and in other countries. It resulted in a number of works on the subject. A controversial book was Hannah Arendt's *Eichmann in Jerusalem*, which describes Eichmann's "banality"—that is, that Eichmann acted like a dull clerk or administrator performing any other routine office job when he planned the destruction of the Jews. By the 1960s, a growing number of DIARIES, memoirs, and testimonies revealed the inner life of European Jews during the Holocaust and balanced the picture presented by the earlier studies. Some of these later works concentrate on Jewish armed RESISTANCE, contradicting the feeling of Jewish passivity.

In the meantime, in SOVIET RUSSIA and other countries under communist rule, there was a clear effort to downplay and even erase the memory of the suffering of Jews *as Jews*. In histories and in memorials, Jews were included in the statistics together with Russians or Poles. This tampering with the numbers served to magnify the suffering of non-Jews (in POLAND one observer noted, "Dead Jews make good Poles"). Efforts were also made to deny the roles of COLLABORATORS among populations of the occupied countries. The roles of the "RIGHTEOUS AMONG THE NATIONS" was exaggerated. Foreign scholars were often denied access to documents. Local historians were not permitted to pursue scholarship that could produce results that went against government positions. As a result, almost nothing was known of the fate of the Jews in Soviet Russia.

This situation changed when communism collapsed. A vast body of documentation was suddenly released. This allowed, for example, the French historian Jean Pressac to publish the first full account of the technical side of the machinery used for mass murder at AUSCHWITZ. Polish historians were finally permitted to do serious research. This new research resulted in changes in the statistics of the number murdered at Auschwitz-Birkenau and the realization of the high proportion of Jews among the victims.

Over the years, historians began to dig into many of the lesser known aspects of the Holocaust and have produced an entire literature on the subject. Many survivors, knowing that the next generation might remain ignorant of the Holocaust, have come forth with accounts of their sufferings. In some cases it was at the urging of children and grandchildren that survivors told their stories. An excellent example of this is Art Spiegelman's *Maus*, which tells the story of his parents' sufferings in comic strip form. Today, the Holocaust is one of the most documented episodes in Jewish history.

The major Holocaust MUSEUMS AND MEMORIALS, including YAD VASHEM, the UNITED STATES HOLOCAUST MEMORIAL MUSEUM, and the GHETTO FIGHTERS' HOUSE, have departments devoted to publishing books on the Holocaust. Detailed surveys of the Holocaust have been published by American historians Lucy Dawidowicz and Nora Levin, Israeli historians Yehuda Bauer and Leni Yahil, and the British historian Sir Martin Gilbert. A major summary of information is in the four-volume *Encyclopedia of the Holocaust*, edited by Yisrael Gutman.

HITLER, ADOLF

(1889–1945) German dictator. He was born in an Austrian village and went to school in the Austrian town of Linz. A poor pupil, at age 18 he went to Vienna to try to fulfil his ambition of becoming a painter. However, he failed the entrance examination at the Academy of Fine Arts and for five years lived off odd jobs and from the sale of sketches and postcards that he painted. He was greatly influenced by the antisemitic ideology of the mayor of Vienna, Karl Lueger. Embracing the dream of German nationalism, he moved to Munich, Germany, in 1913. When World War I broke out, he joined the German army. He found there a sense of security that he had lacked and was a good soldier. At the end of the war, he had the rank of lance-corporal.

After the war, he returned to Munich, bitter over Germany's defeat. Like other antisemites, he could only conclude that Germany had lost because of traitors in its midst—the Jews who had stabbed Germany in the back. Hitler was impressed by the antisemitic German Workers' Party, which was small and unpopular, and he soon became a member of its executive committee. Within two years he was the party leader. He changed the its name to the NATIONAL SOCIALIST GERMAN WORKERS' PARTY (NSDAP)—the NAZI PARTY. Hitler took the title of FÜHRER (leader), instituted the "Heil!" greeting (later "Heil Hitler!") and designed the Nazi flag—a black SWASTIKA on a blood-red background.

The time was ripe for such a party. The German people were disheartened from defeat. Subject to

> *Adolf Hitler is a bloodthirsty guttersnipe, a monster of wickedness, insatiable in his lust for blood and plunder.*
>
> *Winston Churchill*

Hitler delivers a speech in Berlin, 1935

the payment of massive reparations to the Allies as a war punishment, Germany was in an economic crisis. There was extensive unemployment and an inflation which made German money worthless. There was widespread disappointment with the government. By 1923, the Nazi Party had 56,000 members and a private army of 15,000 stormtroopers.

On 8 November 1923, Hitler attempted to take over the Bavarian government in a beer hall in Munich (known as the Beer Hall Putsch). Hitler stood on a chair, pistol in hand, and shouted, "Tomorrow there will be a National Germany or we shall be dead." The Nazis marched to the War Ministry but the revolt collapsed. Hitler was arrested and tried. He used the court as a stage for propaganda and won much sympathy throughout Germany. He was sentenced to five years' imprisonment but was released after a few months. While in prison, he began to write his book MEIN KAMPF, which was to become the Nazi bible.

In the following years, his party continued to grow and the hardships of the great depression brought him more followers. Finally, in the general elections of 1932, the Nazi Party won 230 seats out of 599, making it the largest party—although not with an absolute majority. On 30 January, Hitler was appointed chancellor of Germany. The following month he engineered the burning of the parliament building (the REICHSTAG) and used this as an excuse to crush his left-wing opponents. Soon after, he had

an act passed which brought gave him extensive powers and German democracy to an end.

Now sole dictator, Hitler turned to building up the German army. At the same time, he instituted a regime of fear with police raids and GESTAPO interrogations. In particular, he introduced a series of anti-Jewish regulations designed to exclude the JEWS from German society. At that time, these ranged from the NUREMBERG LAWS to the beginnings of the CONCENTRATION CAMP system. In 1938, he took over AUSTRIA (see ANSCHLUSS), and was granted the Sudetenland region of CZECHOSLOVAKIA in the MUNICH AGREEMENT. In March 1939, he invaded the rest of Czechoslovakia. The rest of the world was becoming alarmed at his aggressions. When he attacked POLAND on 1 September 1939, Britain and FRANCE stood up in Poland's defense and WORLD WAR II broke out. A few days earlier, Hitler had made a pact with his previously bitter enemy, the SOVIET UNION, which kept the latter out of the war at that stage.

Hitler had built up his army to an extraordinary strength, and by virtue of brilliant military tactics he overran Poland in 1939 (see BLITZKRIEG) and most of western Europe in 1940. He seemed unstoppable and was adored by the Germans as the man who had restored their pride. With the conquest of Poland, Hitler began to put into effect his plans for destroying the Jews of Europe.

On 22 June 1941, despite his pact with them, he invaded Russia. Hitler used this attack as an oppor-

The Daily Telegraph

LONDON LATE EDTN.

No. 28,042 LONDON, WEDNESDAY, MAY 2, 1945 and *Morning Post* Printed in LONDON and MANCHESTER PRICE 1½d.

GERMANS ANNOUNCE HITLER'S DEATH

DOENITZ APPOINTED NEW FUEHRER

HIMMLER THROWN OVER: APPEAL TO FIGHT ON

ATTEMPT TO DIVIDE ALLIES: "BOLSHEVISM THE ENEMY"

THE DEATH OF HITLER WAS ANNOUNCED OVER THE GERMAN RADIO SHORTLY BEFORE 10.30 LAST NIGHT. IT SAID THAT IT TOOK PLACE AT HIS COMMAND POST IN BERLIN, NOW ALMOST COMPLETELY OCCUPIED BY RUSSIAN TROOPS.

The announcement said: " It is reported from the Fuehrer's H.Q. that our Fuehrer, Adolf Hitler, has fallen this afternoon at his command post in the Reich Chancellery fighting to the last breath against Bolshevism and for Germany. On Monday the Fuehrer appointed Grand Adml. Doenitz [C.-in-C. of the German Navy] as his successor. Our new

Adolf Hitler, whose death was announced by German radio last night. House painter, corporal, demagogue, dictator. A typical pose. Other pictures on Page 5.

BRITISH THREAT TO LUEBECK

ELBE BRIDGEHEADS LINKED UP

From DOUGLAS WILLIAMS, *Daily Telegraph* Special Correspondent SHAEF, Tuesday.

The bridgeheads across the Elbe, formed by the American and British forces of the British Second Army, have linked up. The united forces are pushing on towards Hamburg and the Baltic port of Luebeck.

Between the British troops and Luebeck there is now a gap of only 18 miles. This means that the tanks of the 11th Armoured Division have covered nearly half the distance between the Elbe and the port.

The narrow gap represents the only remaining escape route for the Germans in all Denmark. Yet many of the enemy forces are moving towards Denmark rather than from it in retreat before the Russians.

R.A.F. fighters attacking a German column 35 miles south-east of Luebeck, destroyed over 100 vehicles and damaged twice as many more.

Redoubt Front

In the south the United States Seventh Army cleared Munich, and south-west of the town are pushing beyond Fuesen into the passes of the Austrian Alps. Other armoured units continue to drive eastwards and are nearing the Inn at Innsbruck and the Brenner Pass.

Gen. Eisenhower has issued an Order of the Day congratulating the Seventh Army on the capture of Munich, "the cradle of the Nazi beast."

The French Army now controls the

KING TO BROADCAST ON VE-DAY

ALL CHURCHES TO BE OPEN, BELLS TO RING

FLOODLIGHTING, BONFIRES AND VICTORY PARADES

The cessation of hostilities in Europe will be announced by the Prime Minister over the wireless, the Home Office stated last night. At nine p.m. the same day the King will address his people throughout the world.

In a circular letter to local authorities issued last night the Home Office expressed the Government's views on the form that national celebrations should take.

The letter said that the arrangements might be subject to revision if the end of hostilities took the form

TWO ARMIES CONVERGE ON BRENNER

of a declaration by the Allied Powers that organised resistance had ceased.

Two Allied forces are converging on the Brenner Pass, Germany's key link with Italy. Striking youth into Austria

Among suggestions made by the Home Office were the following:

Crhurches of all denominations to be open for services and private prayer; church bells will ring

Headline that appeared in The Daily Telegraph newspaper, London, England, announcing Hitler's death

tunity to implement the "FINAL SOLUTION" to the "Jewish question"—their complete extermination. Although no direct order has been found which can be traced to Hitler, there can be no doubt that the "Final Solution" came from him. From the end of 1942, the tide of the war shifted. The Soviet army began to beat back the Germans in the east while the Allies—now joined by the United States—were taking the initiative in the west and south. The worse his military position became, the more desperately Hitler pursued his program of killing the Jews. He set up DEATH CAMPS, where millions were gassed. Convinced of his infallible genius, he blamed his failures on others. Many of his generals sensed defeat and attempted to assassinate him in 1944, but the plot failed.

Eventually, in 1945, the Soviet forces reached the edge of Berlin and the Allied forces were approaching from the other side. Remarkably, Hitler retained the faith of his army and his people to the end. Despite their terrible sufferings, they continued to support him and to fight for him. They had been hypnotized by his speeches and his personality. Only when the end was clearly at hand, Hitler—barricaded in a bunker in Berlin—shot himself. He had come close to becoming the master of the world. Never before had one man committed such terrible crimes.

HITLER YOUTH

(*Hitlerjugend* in German) The youth movement of the NAZI PARTY.

Youth movements were extremely popular and influential in the WEIMAR Republic. Adolf HITLER recognized the power that these organizations had to rally young people around a cause. He was therefore determined to "Nazify" the youth movements of GERMANY. Hitler Youth was first organized in 1926, it had its origins in the Adolf Hitler Boys' Storm Troop founded in 1922. In 1936, Hitler outlawed all other youth groups. By 1938, Hitler Youth grew to include almost 8 million boys and girls from the age of 6 to 21.

The youth movement concerned itself with instilling Nazi ideals, particularly loyalty to the Reich,

In the presence of this blood banner, which represents our Führer, I swear to devote all my energies and my strength to the savior of our country, Adolf Hitler. I am willing and ready to give up my life for him, so help me God.

Oath taken by members of Hitler Youth

militarism, physical activity, labor, political activism and of course, extreme hatred of Jews. Huge gatherings of youth carrying Nazi banners and marching in military formations were carefully planned by the Hitler Youth leadership. Their aim was to create fiercely loyal and racially "pure" manpower for Hitler's Germany. By the time the youth program had taken final shape, the Nazis could supervise German children and youth from the age of 6 through 21 in a wide range of activities which were viewed as even more important than their formal education.

Children aged 6 to 10 entered a preparatory junior youth program. A performance booklet was kept for each child to record his or her physical and ideological achievements. Teenage boys went on to more advanced training. The most talented were later selected for special training for Nazi Party leadership. Teenage girls also received military and other physical training and instruction in Nazi thought. In their case, the emphasis was on their future role as mothers of the ARYAN race. At age 18, when boys entered the Labor Service or the Army, girls joined the B.D.M. (League of German Maidens). They were sent to work on farms and in city households. The many pregnancies of unmarried B.D.M. girls were seen by officials as a positive sign—young women were doing their duty of bearing children for Germany. Parents who objected to their children's participation in these groups had no legal right to prevent it. With the enactment of the "Youth Service Ordinance" of 25 March 1939, participation became mandatory. Thus all German youth were prepared to assume their future role in the Nazi plan.

H L I N K A   G U A R D

Militia in SLOVAKIA. The Hlinka Guard was established by the pro-Nazi Slovak People's Party in 1938 after the signing of the MUNICH AGREEMENT in 1938. It was named for Andrej Hlinka, a Slovak nationalist leader and Catholic clergyman who died in 1938. The Guard operated from 1938 to 1945. Members received paramilitary training and opposed JEWS, Czechs, and supporters of the Left. They wore special black uniforms and used the Nazi salute.

The Hlinka Guard and the Nazis shared a com-

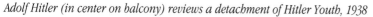

Adolf Hitler (in center on balcony) reviews a detachment of Hitler Youth, 1938

mon interest. The Slovak nationalists wanted independence from CZECHOSLOVAKIA. Adolf HITLER wanted to weaken Czechoslovakia as a potential wartime enemy.

After GERMANY occupied the rest of Czechoslovakia in March 1939, it encouraged Slovakia's independence. Karol Sidor, the Hlinka Guard's commander, was named premier of Slovakia. Alexander Mach took over as commander of the Guard. Its members attacked Jews and destroyed synagogues and Jewish cemeteries.

The Hlinka Guard collaborated with the Nazis in deporting the Jews of Slovakia. As early as 1942, its members collaborated in capturing Jews. However, in 1944, the Vatican representative to Slovakia called on Catholic leaders to speak out against the DEPORTATIONS. This led the Hlinka Guard to stop participating in such actions. After the SLOVAK NATIONAL UPRISING of August 1944, the Hlinka Guard was taken over by the SS.

H O L L A N D

see NETHERLANDS, THE.

H O L O C A U S T

In the English-speaking world, "The Holocaust" is the name given to the systematic, state-sponsored murder of 6 million JEWS by the Nazis and their collaborators during WORLD WAR II. The word comes from the Greek translation of the Hebrew word *olah*, meaning a burnt-offering offered up whole to the Lord in the ancient Temple and completely destroyed. It was not the first name given to the murder of Jews. The Germans called their program of murder "the FINAL SOLUTION to the Jewish Problem." Their intention was to end what they called the "Jewish Problem" forever by eliminating Jews from the world—murdering all Jews. Yiddish-speaking Jews used the word *churban*, destruction, which is the word used for the destruction of the First and Second Temples in 586 B.C.E. and 70 C.E. In Hebrew, the word SHOAH is used, meaning a whirlwind of destruction. Historian Lucy Dawidowicz called the Holocaust "The War Against the Jews," in order to emphasize that the Germans conducted two wars: World War II and the war against the Jews.

The destruction of the Jews was at the center of Nazi beliefs, but Jews were not the only victims. Nazi RACISM was directed against a variety of types of people. Trade unionists and political opponents, Jehovah's Witnesses, and German male HOMOSEXUALS were sent to CONCENTRATION CAMPS. In addition to Jews, the Germans systematically killed three groups: mentally retarded, physically handicapped, and emotionally disturbed Germans were the first to be murdered in a so-called "EUTHANASIA PROGRAM." The Nazis considered these groups "unworthy of living." GYPSIES were also killed. They died in the gas chambers as families—men, women, and children. After the invasion of SOVIET RUSSIA in June 1941, SOVIET PRISONERS OF WAR were put to death, mostly by starvation and exposure without shelter to the cold Russian winter. Those who survived the first winter were allowed to work as slave labor. Approximately 3.3 million Soviet prisoners of war died under German rule.

Adolf HITLER, the leader of the NAZI PARTY, and his followers based their ideas on a long tradition of ANTISEMITISM. For them, antisemitism was a matter of race. The enemy was Jewish blood. They attacked not only religious Jews, or those who identified themselves as Jews, even those Jews who had converted to Christianity. They demanded the complete elimination of the Jews. A Jew was guilty not because of the religious beliefs he practiced, or the identity he affirmed, but because of blood.

The Nazi Persecutions. The Nazis came to power when they were elected to the REICHSTAG, the German parliament. Hitler was asked to become head of a coalition government in January 1933. His opponents thought that once in power he would be forced to moderate or to tone down the antisemitic, racist, and dictatorial aspects of the Nazi platform. They soon learned that they were mistaken. Once in office, Hitler spent the first two years gaining absolute power and ridding himself of all political opponents. He demonstrated his determination to rid GERMANY of its Jews early in his regime. He called for the 1 April 1933 boycott of Jewish businesses (see BOYCOTT, ANTI-JEWISH) and ordered a series of laws that restricted Jewish participation in German life.

In 1935, the NUREMBERG LAWS defined the Jews not by religious identity, practices or traditions, but biologically—by the religious affiliation of their grandparents.

Over the next three years, Jewish property was confiscated, civil rights were limited and then violated completely. Homes, businesses, property, synagogues, public institutions, and private possessions were all taken from the Jews. Jewish students were not allowed to attend schools or college. Jews were segregated—they could not sit on park benches, swim in public pools, or ride in certain cars on trains. These restrictions were designed to force Jews to emigrate and make Germany *judenrein* (free of Jews).

Throughout this period of persecution, Jews tried to leave Germany and find haven elsewhere in the world. Other countries did not want to receive Jewish REFUGEES. This was made clear at the July 1938 EVIAN CONFERENCE, which was convened by the UNITED STATES to come up with a world wide solution to the refugee problem. Each nation had its own excuses as to why it would not admit Jews. The Nazis learned an important lesson: the Jews were unwanted. No one would oppose their anti-Jewish policies.

In Germany these policies were developed law by law, decree by decree. They reached their climax in the pogroms of 9–11 November 1938, known as KRISTALLNACHT, in which the synagogues of Germany and Austria were burned, Jewish businesses attacked and looted, and Jewish homes raided. Thirty thousand men, between the ages of 20 and 60, were arrested and sent to concentration camps.

The process of isolating the Jews from society, which had taken five years in Germany, took only months in AUSTRIA, in the Sudetenland (part of CZECHOSLOVAKIA), and in the rest of Czechoslovakia, after Hitler took them over (1938 and 1939).

In September 1939, Germany invaded POLAND and World War II began. Within a month, more than 2 million Polish Jews came under German control. There was no way that so large a population could be forced to leave, and no country would let them in.

Ghettos and War. Jews in German-occupied Poland were forced to live crowded together in closed areas, called GHETTOS. When the Germans invaded western Europe in 1940, CAMPS—later known as transit camps—were set up in those countries. To the Germans, these were temporary measures, until some final policy could be set. Yet the Jews assumed that the ghettos would be their permanent homes—at least until the war was over. They were wrong.

The German Reich (State) continued to increase in size as the Nazis conquered new territories. The NETHERLANDS (Holland), FRANCE, BELGIUM, LUXEMBOURG, DENMARK, and NORWAY were conquered in the spring and summer of 1940. YUGOSLAVIA and GREECE were invaded by the Germans in early 1941. With each expansion, the number of Jews under German control increased. Anti-Jewish policies were immediately imposed.

The "Final Solution." Sometime in the winter of 1940–1941 a policy decision was made by the Nazi leaders to murder all the Jews under German control. It was named "The Final Solution to the Jewish Problem." Those who acted on this policy were certain that they were carrying out Hitler's will and Germany's national destiny.

After the invasion of Poland in 1939, masses of Jews had been shot in many places throughout the country. With the invasion of Russia in 1941, special mobile killing units called EINSATZGRUPPEN entered newly conquered Soviet territory with the German army troops. In town after town, village after village, and even large cities, these men rounded up the Jews, as well as Gypsies and Soviet commissars, and shot them. This process continued as the German army advanced eastward. Then, the killing units returned for a second roundup of those who were still alive. In 1943, special units returned to these areas to dig up the bodies and burn them, in an attempt to destroy evidence of their crimes (see AKTION 1005).

The Nazis looked for a more rapid method of killing. They chose gassing in DEATH CAMPS, where the victims' bodies were then burned in crematoria (see GAS CHAMBERS, GAS VANS, AND CREMATORIA). The model was a factory assembly line. The produce was thousands of dead Jews each and every day.

From Einsatzgruppen to Death Camps. Ghettos were designed to hold Jews until the death camps were opened. At that point, the ghettos became transit camps—stops on the way to a killing center. Railroads were essential to bring the Jews to the death camps (see RAILWAYS). Deportation meant the beginning of a journey to death. It also meant the final end for Jewish communities in cities—large and small—where Jews had resided for centuries. Deportations involved not only Jews from eastern Europe, but also Jews from western Europe who were sent across Europe to their deaths.

The timetable was swift. The policy was adopted officially in January 1942, at the WANNSEE CONFERENCE. Death camps were built that spring. By the summer of 1942, deportations to death camps had begun. By 1943, most of the Jews who were killed in the Holocaust were already dead.

Three camps were reserved especially for killing Jews: SOBIBÓR, TREBLINKA and BELZEC. AUSCHWITZ-Birkenau and MAJDANEK were three camps in one: killing centers, FORCED LABOR camps, and concentration camps. At Auschwitz, the largest and most deadly of the camps, 1.25 million people were murdered, mostly Jews. Twenty thousand Gypsies were also killed there as well as tens of thousands of Poles and Soviet prisoners of war. A German map of 1945 lists 3,000 camps, but there probably were many more. Forced labor and concentration camps were not solely dedicated to killing. However, conditions were so harsh, the labor so intense, and the food so scarce, that hundreds of thousands of inmates died or were killed. Nazi doctors, such as Josef MENGELE, performed cruel MEDICAL EXPERIMENTS on the inmates.

Upon arrival at Auschwitz, Jews faced selection (see SELEKZIA). An SS physician would divide the young and the able-bodied from other prisoners. Those selected to die would be sent directly to the gas chambers. Their personal possessions were confiscated, and their hair shaved. As many as 2,000 would be sent into the sealed gas chambers at one time. SS personnel would pour two canisters of ZYKLON B poisonous gas down an opening and within 20 to 30 minutes the new arrivals would be dead. Their bodies would then be sent to the crematoria, where gold teeth were removed. When the crematoria could not handle such large numbers, bodies were burned in open fires.

Those who survived the first selection were processed. They would have their hair cut, their property taken, and a number tattooed on their forearm. They lost their names and would be referred to by numbers. They were forced to work for long hours, under harsh conditions. From time to time, prisoners faced selection again. Only the few able to withstand these horrible conditions survived. Weakened or sick prisoners were sent back to Birkenau and gassed.

The fate of Jews differed country by country, region by region. Anti-Jewish measures, which evolved slowly in Germany over 12 years or in Poland over 3 years, took less than 3 months in HUNGARY. The Germans invaded Hungary in March 1944. Jews were singled out immediately and their property was confiscated. By April, they were put in ghettos. On 15 May, the deportation began, and by 8 July, 437,402 Jews had been deported to Auschwitz on 148 trains. Almost all were gassed upon arrival.

Resistance. Groups of Jews fought the Nazis in the forests of eastern Europe and in the ghettos of Poland. They fought as part of mixed RESISTANCE groups in France and Yugoslavia. They fought alone in Poland, and resisted alongside Soviet PARTISANS.

Even in the shadows of the gas chambers, in the death camps of Auschwitz-Birkenau, Treblinka, and Sobibór, Jews managed armed resistance. Crematoria were blown up, and escapes were organized.

Armed resistance was not the first response. Jews had more experience in the art of spiritual resistance, challenging Nazi intentions by non-violent means. Courage in the face of death took many forms. Mothers protected their children, and religious Jews continued to hold services even in concentration camps, some rabbis stayed with their congregations, and great teachers—such as Janusz KORCZAK—stayed with their children to face deportation together.

Those who fought did not imagine that they would win. The odds against them were overwhelming. Unlike classical guerrilla fighters, Jews were confined to ghettos. They were hungry, weak, captive, and vulnerable to Nazi revenge. Thousands could be killed for one single act of resistance. Since antisemitism was widespread, Jewish fighters were endangered even when the population opposed German occupation. All could be killed for the decisions of a few. It was difficult and dangerous to obtain weapons. Armed resistance was an act of desperation. The fighters burned with the desire to protect Jewish honor, to avenge Jewish death.

Acts of extraordinary courage by individual non-Jews, who put their own lives in danger by sheltering and hiding Jews took place in many countries. They were only a minority of the population, but they saved the lives of tens of thousands of Jews (see "RIGHTEOUS AMONG THE NATIONS").

World War II and the War against the Jews. The progress of World War II affected the Holocaust. As the Nazi empire expanded, more Jews came under Nazi control. When the Germans knew that defeat was near and that they had to retreat, the pace of killing often increased so they could kill all the Jews before pulling out. Each area liberated from German control brought relief to its population, but in most cases few Jews remained alive.

In the final months of the war, just before the death camps of eastern Europe were captured by Soviet forces, the Nazis began a series of DEATH MARCHES. These were forced evacuations of the camp inmates by foot and by rail. They were hasty retreats to get the victims away from their liberators, to silence the living eyewitnesses. Few, if any, provisions were supplied. There was no food, no place to sleep, no way to keep warm. For the victims, the struggle was no longer against the Nazis, but against death itself. In their weakened conditions, they were forced to draw upon their remaining strength, beyond the limits of endurance.

As the Allied armies swept through Europe in 1944 and 1945, they found 7 to 9 million DISPLACED PERSONS of many nationalities living in countries not their own. More than 6 million returned to their native lands. However, more than 1 million refused to go back. Victims became displaced persons, with no country, in search of new homes and new lands.

There was nowhere to go for the hundreds of thousands of Jews who survived. They were without homes. Their communities had been destroyed. Often they were the last living members of their family. The presence of so many Jews on German soil, living among their former killers, forced world leaders to work to find a place for the Jews to go—but without opening the doors of their own countries. Most survivors wanted to go to PALESTINE, where they could live among Jews, hopefully in an independent Jewish state. But the British blocked their entry, so the Jews attempted two types of "illegal" immigration: BERIHA, an escape from Soviet-held territories to U. S. or British-held territories, and ALIYA BET, the attempt to move from Europe to Palestine, which

was against British policy. Only in 1948, when the State of ISRAEL was proclaimed, could its shores open to receive the Jews. Then most did find a home, a place to rebuild their lives.

What of the killers? In the winter of 1943, President Franklin D. ROOSEVELT, British Prime Minister Winston CHURCHILL, and Russian leader Joseph STALIN declared their intention to bring Nazi leaders to trial in a court of justice. After the discovery of the concentration camps, the drive to prosecute Nazi war criminals increased.

Just after the war ended and shortly after President Harry S. TRUMAN came to office, he asked Supreme Court Justice Robert Jackson to lead the U. S. effort. Nuremberg, the site of annual Nazi Party parades, was chosen as the location for the trials of Nazi war criminals.

There were two series of trials at NUREMBERG, and over the past 50 years, the TRIALS OF WAR CRIMINALS have continued because of the unparalleled nature of their crimes. In 1948, the United Nations passed the GENOCIDE CONVENTION, which was designed to overcome the claims of Nazi defendants that they had violated no law.

The convention specifically defined the various aspects of Nazi murder as crimes. It declared as illegal the killing of persons belonging to a group (the "Final Solution"); causing bodily or spiritual harm to members of a group; deliberately enforcing upon the group living conditions that could lead to complete or partial destruction (ghettos and starvation); enforcing measures to prevent births among the group (STERILIZATION); forcibly removing children from the group and transferring them to another group (the ARYANIZATION of Polish children). The adoption of the convention was followed the next day by the adoption of a Universal Declaration of Human Rights.

HOLOCAUST AND JEWISH THOUGHT

While the Holocaust was still raging, Jews asked, "How could God be allowing this to happen?" This question has continued to concern Jewish thinkers. Going back to the message of the biblical prophets, some rabbis have suggested that it was a punishment for the Jews' failure to live up to God's demands. However, most philosophers and theologians reject the idea that the Holocaust was in any way a divine punishment. Yet they admit that it was a supreme test of faith.

The Bible portrays an example of tragic suffering that is not punishment for sin. In the book of Job, the hero protests the personal pain and agony that he does not deserve. In the end, Job recognizes that man simply cannot understand the ways of God. In modern times, some give the same answer to the Holocaust.

Martin Buber, a Jewish philosopher, spoke of an "eclipse of God." Developing an ancient Jewish concept, he writes that on occasion, God withdraws His face from humankind. Even so, writes Buber, God is always present despite the apparent absence of His influence at AUSCHWITZ. Leo BAECK, the German rabbi who survived the THERESIENSTADT CONCENTRATION CAMP, emerged with hope. He still believed deeply in the Jewish capacity for rebirth. He saw the rise of the State of ISRAEL from the ashes of Auschwitz as the most meaningful expression of this rebirth. Indeed, there have been many Jews who have seen Israel as the answer to the Holocaust. However, others are not satisfied with this. They ask if 6 million people had to be destroyed to justify the Jewish State.

Other thinkers insist that the unparalleled nature of the Holocaust calls for completely new ways of thinking. The American Richard Rubenstein writes that the Holocaust brings the existence of God into question. However, at the same time, Rubenstein believes in a meaningful future, learning from Auschwitz that life is the supreme value.

The German-born philosopher Emil Fackenheim was himself in a concentration camp before the war. He has identified a new divine commandment that comes out of the DEATH CAMP: the Jewish people must survive so as not to hand victory over to Adolf HITLER after his death. An American rabbi, Irving Greenberg, learns from the Holocaust that powerlessness is immoral because it does not ensure survival. He too sees in the founding of the State of Israel a redeeming act following the great catastrophe. Greenberg feels that the answer to Auschwitz can be found in acts of love and lifegiving.

A further group of responses finds the answer in the free will that God gives to human beings, who can choose evil as well as good. The American theologian Arthur A. Cohen concludes that God does not have the power to interfere in human affairs. What some call God's speech is really always man's hearing. Several thinkers maintain that condemning the Holocaust as an absolute evil involves acknowledging that there is absolute good. This confirms the traditional Jewish call to goodness.

A final reaction to the Holocaust is—silence. The French André Neher writes that Auschwitz was silence—the silence of those who understood what was happening and the silence of God. The Israeli thinker Pinchas Peli notes that the language of religion is filled with meaningful silences. American theologian Abraham Joshua Heschel finds that the lesson of the Holocaust is for man to take action against surrounding evils. However, man does not have the right to question God about human suffering: in God's presence, man must remain silent.

HOLOCAUST DENIAL

The claim that the Holocaust is a myth which never happened; that its size has been widely exaggerated; or that it was not an unusual event in human history (see HOLOCAUST, UNIQUENESS OF). Because no order written by Adolf HITLER himself has been discovered that says that the Jews should be murdered, some even claim that the Holocaust took place without Hitler's knowledge.

This type of thinking began even before the war ended, despite all the physical evidence that contradicted it. There were the survivors, the Allied soldiers who entered the CAMPS, the photographs and movies of the horrors they found, and much other confirming evidence. Unbelievably, Holocaust denials (which should seem ridiculous to all) are still taken seriously by some individuals and groups in various parts of the world.

The NUREMBERG TRIAL examined German documents and heard from top Nazi officials. These confirmed the details of the entire plan and execution of the "FINAL SOLUTION." Yet still Holocaust denial made headway. For example, in the United States, a California group called the Institute for Historical Review was founded in 1978. Members called themselves "revisionist historians." They took the name from an accepted school of historians to make themselves sound more reliable. Other pseudo-historians who deny the Holocaust have sprung up in many countries—such as CANADA, FRANCE, and South Africa. They often come from or are closely associated with NEO-NAZISM circles (i.e., groups in the postwar world who still favor Nazi ways). They print material, make videos, post their ideas and antisemitic PROPAGANDA on the Internet, appear on radio and television talk shows, and send ads to college campuses. All their materials question the existence or the scope of the Holocaust. They quote facts out of context to make their claims sound reasonable. Some people who lack background, knowledge, and understanding of history actually believe this propaganda.

Various steps have been taken to fightthese lies. In a growing number of countries, Holocaust denial has been outlawed, and those who carry it out are punished. Another approach has been to record the authentic memoirs of survivors (see TESTIMONIES). This way, when those who lived through the Holocaust will no longer be available to speak themselves of what happened, an authentic record will be preserved. Another direction is the development of Holocaust education, especially in schools. This is more than the study of another chapter of history. It is very important for teaching the evils and dangers of ANTISEMITISM and all forms of RACISM and hatred of other groups. It is also a protection against those who, by denying the Holocaust, would see history repeat itself.

H O L O C A U S T
R E M E M B R A N C E D A Y

("Yom ha-Shoah")

Day set aside each year to commemorate the events and victims of the Holocaust.

On 12 April 1951, the Israeli Parliament declared the Hebrew date, 27 Nisan, as the "Holocaust and Ghetto Uprising Remembrance Day—a day of ongoing remembrance for the House of Israel." This date was the anniversary of the WARSAW GHETTO UPRISING. The day is observed in Israel with a siren to mark a nationwide moment of silence. There is a central public commemoration at the Holocaust memorial, YAD VASHEM, attended by the president of Israel. Local memorial ceremonies take place throughout the country. Discussion of the Holocaust and RESISTANCE are held in all schools and in the media. On the eve of the Day, all places of entertainment are closed.

Outside Israel, Holocaust Day is observed on 19 April (the secular date of the Warsaw Ghetto Uprising) or on the Sunday closest to that date. Services are held at local Holocaust memorials. Jewish communities organize public meetings and invite government and community leaders to participate. In synagogues, a memorial prayer is recited for the victims of the Holocaust. In 1996, president Roman Herzog of GERMANY decreed that 27 January, the date of the liberation of AUSCHWITZ, would be the official Remembrance Day in his country. Memorials are also held other in countries where the Nazis murdered Jews. These are generally on the dates when DEPORTATIONS started or when many Jews were killed. In communist countries, the authorities frowned upon these ceremonies. However, since the fall of SOVIET RUSSIA and the other communist regimes, the Holocaust is remembered publicly, often with the involvement of government, community, and church leaders.

H O L O C A U S T
U N I Q U E N E S S O F

In recent years, the term *Holocaust* has come to be carelessly applied to all kinds of GENOCIDE and mass death, such as the "Armenian holocaust," "the Cambodian holocaust," and the "Rwandan holocaust." This is disturbing to those who feel that a unique event should be described by a unique term.

The special nature of the Holocaust lies in the fact that never before in history has a government set out, as a matter of principle and policy, to murder every man, woman, and child belonging to a specific people. Adolf HITLER said that the NATIONAL SOCIALIST PARTY was more than a religion; it was an attempt to create mankind anew—without the JEWS. This differs from anything else the world has known. Earlier, ANTISEMITISM never aimed for the complete destruction of the Jews. There have been terrible massacres by the conquistadors in the Americas and of the native American Indians, but there was never a conscious intent to eliminate them. The loss of life in modern times, in places like Cambodia and Rwanda, has not been motivated by total genocide. The same can be said of the Turkish massacre of Armenians in 1917, during

World War I. Even the Nazi treatment of GYPSIES, HOMOSEXUALS, and the Slavic nations was not based on a policy of total destruction. The Holocaust was a unique event. For this reason, many believe that the use of the word *Holocaust* should be restricted to the fate of the Jews at the hands of the Nazis.

HOMOSEXUALS

Even though homosexuality had been outlawed in GERMANY for centuries, it was tolerated in the years before the Nazis rose to power. Books in favor of homosexuality had been published and there were gay bars in major cities.

Soon after Adolf HITLER took office, however, he banned all homosexual groups. In 1933, the pro-homosexual Institute for Sexual Research was vandalized. Stormtroopers were raiding gay bars; homosexuals were being imprisoned and marked with yellow bands with the letter 'A'.

In June 1934, Hitler arranged the murder of his faithful lieutenant Ernst RÖHM, a known homosexual, and 300 of Röhm's men, some of them also homosexuals. Shortly after, Heinrich HIMMLER created a special criminal police office to fight homosexuality. By December 1934, homosexual "intent" was a crime and many homosexuals were sent to CONCENTRATION CAMPS.

The Nazis felt that although lesbianism was "alien to German women...even lesbian wombs could breed." Thus, while there was some discrimination, lesbians were not deliberately persecuted and arrested.

Only German homosexual men were persecuted. Homosexuals in the occupied territories were merely labeled inferior. Their sexual orientation was seen as a threat to breeding the Aryan "master race," but since their status as Aryans was never in question, they were not targeted for systematic murder.

In the concentration camps, homosexuals were identified by a pink triangular BADGE and subjected to harsh treatment. They were also badly treated by other camp inmates and thousands died.

Since homosexuality was still outlawed in Germany after the war, homosexuals were afraid to speak up and report on their experience in the camps.

HORST WESSEL LIED

("Horst Wessel's Song")

Marching song of the SA and the second national anthem of the THIRD REICH (after *Deutschland über Alles*—"Germany Over All"). The lyrics come from a poem by Horst Wessel, an SA member, who was shot to death in a brawl with the communists in 1930. Josef GOEBBELS seized the opportunity to turn Wessel's death into a political assassination and make him a martyr to the Nazi cause. Books and a film soon depicted Wessel as a hero.

HORTHY, MIKLÓS

(1868–1957) Ruler of HUNGARY. In World War I, he served in the Austro-Hungarian navy, rising to the rank of rear admiral. In 1920, he took over the government of Hungary and adopted the title of regent. His right-wing, antisemitic government established discriminatory laws, including the *Numerus Clausus* law of 1920, the first in postwar Europe to limit the number of Jews who could be admitted to universities.

After Hungary joined the Rome-Berlin Axis in 1934, he followed the example of Nazi GERMANY by passing ANTI-JEWISH LAWS of increasing severity. However, he refused to bend to pressure from Adolf HITLER to introduce even more extreme measures such as building ghettos and deporting Jews. Horthy was summoned to go to Hitler on 18 March 1944 and was told that his country would be occupied by German troops the next day. He accepted a completely pro-Nazi government, which would deport half a million Jews from Hungary. On 19 July 1944, with Russian troops already inside Hungary's borders, he responded to the calls of the king of Sweden, the RED CROSS, and the Vatican to halt the deportations. Nevertheless, deportations were started again on 4 August.

At the end of August, Horthy appointed General Géza Lakatos as prime minister. Lakatos renewed attempts to get Hungary out of the war. When Horthy's son was kidnapped by the Nazis in October 1944, Horthy announced an armistice with the Allies. He was overthrown within hours, to be replaced by Ferenc SZÁLASI, who collaborated completely with the Nazis. Horthy was confined by the

Horst Wessel

Germans until 1945. He was held until 1948 by the Americans, who refused to extradite him to Hungary and released him. He died in exile in Portugal.

HÖSS, RUDOLF

(1900–1947) Commandant of AUSCHWITZ DEATH CAMP. On Heinrich HIMMLER's instructions, Höss developed Auschwitz from a CONCENTRATION CAMP into the largest center for the mass murder of European Jewry.

Höss became an active member of the SS in 1934.

> *I was a cog in the wheel of the great extermination machine created by the Third Reich. The machine has been smashed to pieces, the engine is broken, and I "too must now be" destroyed. The world demands it.*

conclusion of Höss's autobiography, 1947

He gained experience in running concentration camps at DACHAU and SACHSENHAUSEN. After the Nazis conquered POLAND in September 1939, the SS saw the area as an ideal place to imprison those whom they viewed as "enemies" of the THIRD REICH. Höss was assigned to investigate the possibility of converting some old Polish army barracks near the town of Auschwitz into a concentration camp. He was appointed commandant of the new camp in May 1940.

The camp quickly grew to house around 40,000 inmates. In May 1941, Himmler ordered Höss to establish a camp for 100,000 prisoners at nearby Brzezinka. This new camp became known as Auschwitz II, or Birkenau. It became the center of the killing operations in the summer of 1941. That was when Himmler informed Höss of Adolf HITLER's order that Auschwitz was to play a special role in the "FINAL SOLUTION" to the "Jewish question." Auschwitz was chosen because of its convenient location.

After some experimentation, Höss decided that ZYKLON B gas was the most effective means for mur-

Detention card of Miklós Horthy as a war criminal

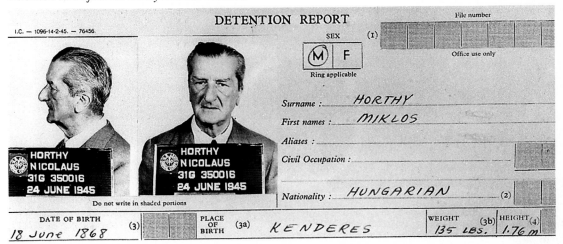

Rudolf Höss as a prisoner in Kraków jail, 1946

dering masses of people at the greatest possible speed. As a witness at the postwar NUREMBERG TRIAL, he boasted of the improvements in the killing process, that he had made over the techniques employed at TREBLINKA, where carbon monoxide was used. From the summer of 1941 to November 1943, Höss was in charge of the murder at Auschwitz of Jewish communities from Poland, FRANCE, the NETHERLANDS, GREECE, BOHEMIA AND MORAVIA, SLOVAKIA, BELGIUM, GERMANY, AUSTRIA, YUGOSLAVIA, ITALY, NORWAY, and BULGARIA.

In November 1943, Höss was transferred to Berlin to work for the SS Economic and Administrative Main Office. Nevertheless, he returned to Auschwitz in the summer of 1944 to supervise personally the murder of more than 400,000 Hungarian Jews. At the trials at Nuremberg, he claimed to have presided over the gassing of 2.5 million Jews. Later, and more accurately, he claimed that this figure was 1.13 million. In March 1947, the Supreme National Tribunal of Poland sentenced Höss to death, and he was hanged the following month.

H U N G A R Y

State in eastern Europe. Hungary was ruled from 1920 by Admiral Miklós HORTHY, who joined the Nazi-Fascist alliance in 1940. He declared war on the SOVIET UNION, GREAT BRITAIN, and FRANCE in 1941. As a reward, GERMANY gave Hungary huge tracts of land from its neighbors. In 1941, Hungary had 825,000 JEWS. The first anti-Jewish law, passed by parliament in May 1938, limited the number of Jewish wage-earners in the population to 20 percent. A second law, passed later that year, reduced Jewish workers to 6 percent. In 1941, anti-Jewish laws similar to the NUREMBERG LAWS were passed in Hungary. The Jewish community lost its right to collect taxes, Jews were barred from the professions, and agricultural land owned by Jews was confiscated in 1942.

Between July 1939 and November 1940, 52,000 Jewish men, aged 18 to 48, were drafted into labor

Entrance to the ghetto of Mukacevo (Munkács), Hungary, 1944

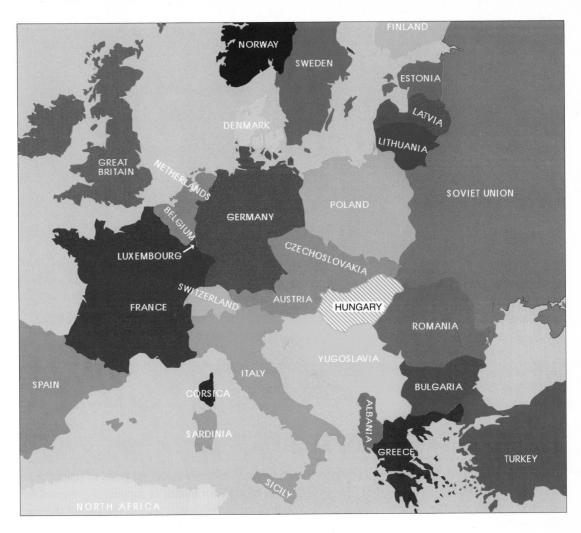

battalions. They received inhuman treatment from sadistic army officers. An additional 50,000 were sent to the UKRAINE to build roads, repair fortifications, and clear mine fields. It is estimated that by March 1944, 42,000 of them had died of hunger, typhoid and the hazards of war.

In the summer of 1941, 35,000 Jews were rounded up and imprisoned, accused of being unable to prove their Hungarian citizenship. Twenty-five thousand were handed over to the Germans, who shot most of them. Other Jews were sent to salt mines in labor battalions. By 1944, the remaining Jewish population consisted mostly of children under 18 and adults over 50. They were severely impoverished and underfed.

On 19 March 1944, the Germans marched into Hungary and set up a puppet government. Adolf EICHMANN went to BUDAPEST to organize the murder of Jews remaining in Hungary. All Jews outside Budapest were forced into GHETTOS. From May to July 1944, 435,000 Jews from all over the country were sent to their deaths in AUSCHWITZ.

In July 1944, Horthy stopped the DEPORTATIONS of Jews and arranged an armistice with the Soviet Union. However, before it could be signed, the Germans arrested him. In October 1944, they installed a government headed by the pro-Nazi ARROW CROSS party. Prominent leaders and professionals were taken 'hostage' and sent to DEATH CAMPS. More than 70,000 men and women went on a cruel DEATH MARCH to be used as forced laborers in Nazi CONCENTRATION CAMPS and to build fortifications. Thousands were shot into the Danube river. Thousands more died of hunger and disease in the Budapest ghetto, into which 70,000 Jews were crowded. Thanks to the efforts of Zionist groups and of neutral diplomats,

Jews in Budapest were permitted to shop only during specified periods during the day

140,000 Jews survived the 10-month Nazi occupation of Hungary. Over 620,000 Hungarian Jews had been killed.

HUSSEINI, HAJJ AMIN AL

(1893–1974) Palestinian-Arab leader and Nazi collaborator. Husseini led riots against Jews in Jerusalem in April 1920. He used his post as Grand Mufti (Muslim religious leader) of Jerusalem to provoke Arabs to acts of violence against Jews in PALESTINE. In 1937, he was dismissed from his post and escaped to Damascus. An early sympathizer with Nazi GERMANY, Husseini and his movement received financial aid from Germany. At the outbreak of WORLD WAR II, Husseini fled to IRAQ, where he took an active part in the pro-Nazi uprising organized by Rashid Ali in 1941. With the defeat of Ali, Husseini fled first to ITALY and later to Germany. In November 1941, he met with Adolf HITLER. Husseini's goals were to secure German aid for Arab nationalism and to encourage the extermination of European Jewry. Most of his high-flown plans came to nothing. However, he was able to provide the Germans with intelligence information and helped in promoting Nazism in the Arab world.

In 1943, Husseini recruited a Muslim unit of 20,000 men in CROATIA, which fought with the Yugoslav partisans and participated in a number of massacres. From the end of 1942, he repeatedly urged the German air force to bomb Tel-Aviv (the city had been subjected to several Italian air raids in 1941). He also called for the Jews of Tripoli in LIBYA to be killed before the German retreat. Husseini vigorously lobbied against all plans to release Jews in exchange for money or supplies. He pressed for their complete destruction. At the end of the war, Husseini fell into French hands but escaped to Cairo. From there he continued to work on behalf of the Arab cause. He played an active role in Arab affairs until his death.

The Mufti Hajj al-Amin Husseini shakes hands with Nazi leaders during a visit to Germany

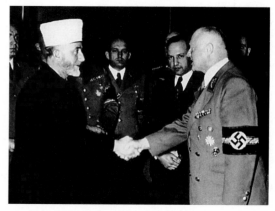

I A S I

see JASSY.

I. G. FARBEN

German dye and chemical company, established in 1925 and based in Frankfurt on Main. The members of the management were early and enthusiastic supporters of Adolf HITLER and the NAZI PARTY. They contributed enormous sums of money to the party between 1933 and 1944.

I.G. Farben received a great deal of looted Jewish property from the countries occupied by GERMANY. It was also one of the largest employers of CONCENTRA-TION CAMP labor. Its artificial rubber and synthetic gasoline plants were in the AUSCHWITZ camp complex.

Tens of thousands of prisoners were worked to death in those plants. The average life span for prisoners there was three months. I.G. Farben staff actively participated in MEDICAL EXPERIMENTS on concentration camp prisoners, attempting to develop various means of STERILIZATION. ZYKLON B, the chemical agent used in the GAS CHAMBERS of Auschwitz, was developed by I.G. Farben and produced by two private firms, one controlled by I.G. Farben.

IMMIGRATION ("Illegal")

see ALIYA BET.

I. G. Farben factory, in Monowitz, Auschwitz, Poland

I R A Q

Middle Eastern country. When Iraq became independent in 1932, the Jewish community of some 120,000 was relatively well integrated. In Baghdad, the capital, Jews made up a quarter of the inhabitants. After 1932, their situation grew steadily worse for two reasons: one was the rise of Arab nationalism due to increased Jewish settlement in PALESTINE. Another was intense propaganda efforts by GERMANY trying to rally Iraq to its side. A series of discriminatory measures—firing of Jewish civil servants and bank employees, restriction on the number of JEWS admitted to schools and universities—were followed by attacks on the Jewish population. On the eve of the Jewish New Year in 1936, three Jews were assassinated and on Yom Kippur a bomb exploded in the great synagogue of Baghdad. In April 1941, a group of pro-Nazi colonels seized power and anti-Jewish rioting broke out. During the few weeks of their antisemitic campaign they roused the populace and put fear into the Jewish community. An attack on the Jews left 179 dead and 2,118 wounded. In a series of shocking incidents infants were massacred, women raped and synagogues desecrated. In May, British troops took over the country and the situation calmed down. The scars left by that period caused the entire Jewish population of Iraq to leave for ISRAEL in the early 1950s.

I R O N   G U A R D

FASCIST organization in ROMANIA. In 1923, Alexandru C. Cuza, a Romanian nationalist antisemitic leader, founded the National Christian Defense League. It called for removing Jews from Romanian public life. In 1927, another antisemitic group, the Legion of the Archangel Michael, was established by Corneliu Zelea Codreanu and other nationalist students. The Legion was responsible for attacks on Jews, in Oradea-Mare, Cluj and other Romanian towns.

In 1929–1930, the two groups merged to form the Iron Guard. In 1933, the Iron Guard was disbanded by the liberal premier, Ion Duca. Three weeks later, the Guard had Duca shot and the movement was reestablished. After the Nazis came to power in GERMANY, the Guard established ties with them.

In 1938, Romania's King Carol became fearful of the increasing power of the Guard. The king had Codreanu imprisoned and killed, supposedly while he was trying to escape. In the summer of 1940, a deal was made between the King and the Guard. As a result, the leader of the Iron Guard, Horia Sima, entered the government led by Ion ANTONESCU. A wave of terrorism against Jews was launched immediately.

On 21 January 1941, the Iron Guard revolted against the government. The Guard stirred up a pogrom in BUCHAREST, which lasted for 3 days and claimed the lives of 121 Jews. Many of the victims were killed in an animal slaughterhouse. Their bodies were hung from hooks and marked "kosher meat." Hundreds of shops, businesses and homes were looted, 25 synagogues were desecrated and hundreds of Jews were raped and beaten. The pogrom was finally crushed by Antonescu, and most of the Iron Guard leaders sought refuge in Germany. After the war, Horia Sima escaped to SPAIN. The Iron Guard still claims a following among Romanians living in North and South America and elsewhere. Since the collapse of communism, sympathizers have also appeared in Romania itself.

I S R A E L ,   S T A T E   O F

Jewish state in the Middle East. On 14 May 1948, just three years after the liberation of the CONCENTRATION CAMPS in Eastern Europe, the modern State of Israel was born. Many historians have made a close connection between the two events. They say that there is a clear cause-and-effect relationship between the Holocaust and the rise of the State of Israel. Others say that a Jewish state would have eventually arisen anyway, despite the objections of the Arabs. However, the extraordinary suffering of Jews during the HOLOCAUST stepped up the process that led to Israel's creation.

The Holocaust and the difficulties of the DISPLACED PERSONS after the war inspired furious efforts on the part of the Jews in PALESTINE to rescue Jews from Europe. They were determined to establish their own state to provide a home for the many survivors still in camps, mostly in GERMANY, whom the countries of the world were unwilling to admit.

The impact of the Holocaust on the United Na-

Children Holocaust survivors arriving in Haifa on board an Israeli ship, October 1948

tions decision of 29 November 1947 to create the State of Israel is also clear. While the major powers—the UNITED STATES, SOVIET RUSSIA and FRANCE—found it in their own best interest to support a Jewish state, the Holocaust and the situation of the displaced persons played a special role in their decisions.

The Holocaust is important in everyday life and thought in Israel. Thousands of survivors immigrated to the new state in 1948 and 1949. Many more followed in succeeding years. The impact of the Holocaust on the consciousness of Israelis became particularly strong under the impact of the Eichmann Trial (see EICHMANN, ADOLF). The national day of mourning for Holocaust victims is HOLOCAUST MEMORIAL DAY, which includes a nationwide moment of silent reflection, special classes in all schools, special programming on television and radio and visits to the country's Holocaust museums—notably YAD VASHEM in Jerusalem and the GHETTO FIGHTERS' HOUSE in Galilee.

ISTANBUL RESCUE COMMITTEE OF THE JEWISH AGENCY

see JEWISH AGENCY .

I T A L Y

Country in southern Europe. The HOLOCAUST in Italy was different both in length and intensity from the experience of most European countries during WORLD WAR II. One reason for this was that German forces did not occupy Italy until late in the war. However, several other unusual factors in Italy help to explain the survival of nearly 85 percent of Italy's 45,200 JEWS.

ANTISEMITISM was never particularly strong in Italian society. When the fascist dictator (see FASCISM AND FASCIST MOVEMENTS), Benito MUSSOLINI came to power in 1922, antisemitism was not part of his program. Jews were only a small fraction of the whole population and were generally well integrated into Italian society. They had important positions in the civil

service, military, and professions. Many Jews even joined the Fascist Party, since they supported its objectives.

Changes for the worse began in 1936, when Italy joined GERMANY in the Spanish Civil War (see glossary). Mussolini was trying to build closer relations with Adolf HITLER's Germany. Mussolini started an anti-Jewish PROPAGANDA campaign in an effort to develop popular support for the persecution of Italy's Jews. In September 1938, Fascist Italy introduced its first ANTI-JEWISH LEGISLATION.

The racial laws of 1938 isolated the Jews from the rest of Italian society. Marriage between Jews and non-Jews was banned, and Jews were prohibited from serving in the army or joining the Fascist Party. Restrictions were placed on Jewish ownership of land and businesses. Jews were removed

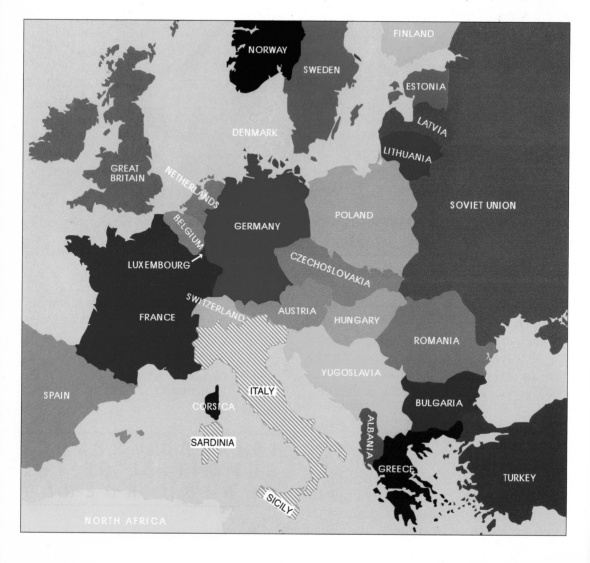

from Italian professional and educational life. In 1939 and 1940, additional racial laws were passed which classified Jewish refugees in Italy as "enemy aliens" and authorized their arrest by Italian police. Thousands were imprisoned in Italian CONCENTRATION CAMPS, which had been built to house Mussolini's opponents. Conditions in these camps were poor. There was no adequate housing, food, or water, and disease was widespread. However, life in Italian concentration camps was not nearly as bad as in German camps. Prisoners were often allowed to maintain schools for their children, form orchestras, and use camp libraries. Men and women were separated, but mothers were allowed to care for their children and for any orphans in the camp. The exception was La Risiera de San Sabba, a factory that had been turned into a prison. It was equipped with a crematorium (SEE GAS CHAMBERS, GAS VANS, AND CREMATORIA) by the men of the SS who had overseen the establishment of the DEATH CAMPS in POLAND. Here the staff was extremely cruel, and life was more like that in German concentration camps.

In 1943, the Allies landed in southern Italy and began to move northward. The Mussolini regime was overthrown. His successors signed a treaty with the Allies on 8 September. This was the signal for the Germans to reoccupy all parts of the country that the Allies had not reached, which included ROME. The Germans established a puppet government under Mussolini. With the Germans in control, the most brutal period of the Holocaust soon began for Italian Jews.

A full scale search for Jews began. Violence against the Jewish population grew as Italian antisemites and SS men took advantage of the new circumstances. Theodor Dannecker, the SS commander in Italy, seized lists of Jewish residents from local Italian police. Throughout September, 1943, he prepared to arrest and deport the Jews in many Italian cities. Fortunately, many were able to go into

Adolf Hitler (right) visiting Benito Mussolini in Venice

hiding with the help of the Catholic Church (see CHRISTIAN CHURCHES) and the anti-German Italian population.

The first searches of Rome, Trieste, Milan, Turin, and other cities in October turned up few Jews. Nevertheless, the SS, aided by Italian COLLABORATORS, persisted. By April 1945, it had successfully deported almost 7,000 Jews to their deaths in AUSCHWITZ and other German camps.

The great majority of Jews in Italy survived the war. This shows what was possible when the native population did not sympathize with Nazi aims. Like the Danes (see DENMARK), many Italians courageously risked their lives to save strangers.

j

J A N Ó W S K A

Nazi LABOR and DEATH CAMP on Janówska Road in LVOV, on the site of a formerly Jewish-owned factory. In September 1941, using Jewish forced labor, the Germans established an armaments factory there. By October, the number of Jewish prisoners working in Janówska had reached 600 and the factory was turned into a CONCENTRATION CAMP. The prisoners primarily did wood and metal work, but the Germans also forced them to perform purposeless tasks designed to exhaust them. The head of the Lvov JUDENRAT refused to turn over more JEWS for forced labor in the camp and he was executed by the Nazis.

In March 1942, when deportations of Jews from East Galicia in southeast POLAND to the BELZEC death camp began, Janówska was used as a transit center. Women, children, the elderly and the ill were immediately sent to their deaths at Belzec, while those capable of heavy work were kept at Janówska. Later, in the spring and summer of 1942, Janówska itself became a death camp. It is difficult to calculate accurately the number of Jews murdered there, but the estimate is several tens of thousands. There were attempts to organize resistance, but these failed. This is probably because the date for closing the camp was moved up suddenly to November 1943, and the prisoners were caught in a state of unreadiness. Even so, one revolt was staged by the so-called SONDERKOMMANDO, and several Nazi guards were killed. Most of the Jews who succeeded in escaping were hunted down and killed.

J A P A N

Country in eastern Asia. During the 1930s, Japan occupied large areas of eastern China. Although there

Circle of musicians, Janówska camp

Hitler receiving a Japanese delegation, 1934

were few JEWS in Japan, many lived in the conquered areas. Over 30,000 Jews came under Japanese control during WORLD WAR II. Fifteen thousand of these were Jews who had been living in eastern China. Seventeen thousand were REFUGEES from Nazi Europe, whom the Japanese allowed to settle in SHANGHAI, which was under their control. In general, the Japanese were not antisemitic. They believed that Jews held a tremendous amount of power in the west. Leading Japanese officials developed a plan in the 1930s to offer refuge to 50,000 Jews in Japanese-controlled China as ANTISEMITISM grew in Europe. In this way they hoped to win American sympathy and attract large sums of Jewish money. Negotiations lasted several years, but the plan came to nothing once the Japanese allied themselves with Nazi GERMANY in 1940.

The Japanese went along with Germany's policy of antisemitism by publishing many antisemitic works in Japanese. At the same time, they were not happy with Adolf HITLER'S RACISM and his belief in the superiority of the "Aryan" race. The conditions of the Jews under their control were not harsh and Jews were allowed to manage their own affairs. After 1943, under German pressure, most but not all Jews in Shanghai had to live in a GHETTO. Life there was not easy due to overcrowding, economic problems, and a shortage of food, but the inhabitants were generally left along. They were not subjected to the horrifying conditions of the ghettos in Eu-

rope. Both Japan and the United States allowed aid to be sent to ghetto residents from Jewish American organizations. The Japanese consul in KOVNO (LITHUANIA), Sempo SUGIHARA, helped Jews escape from Europe to Shanghai.

J A S E N O V A C

The largest of the CONCENTRATION CAMPS set up in CROATIA after it declared its independence under Ante PAVELIC and his USTASHA regime. It was located 626 miles south of Zagreb, the Croatian capital. JEWS from all over the former YUGOSLAVIA were sent there from the time the camp was opened in August 1941 until the summer of 1942, when mass DEPORTATIONS of Jews to AUSCHWITZ began. Political opponents, Serbs and GYPSIES were also imprisoned in Jasenovac. It was intended at first as a FORCED LABOR camp, and skilled workers ran a number of workshops.

Since the fiercely antisemitic Ustasha were in charge of the camp, conditions were particularly harsh. The worst period was the fall and winter of 1942, when a former priest, dubbed Fra Sotona—Brother Satan—was in charge. He was responsible for the deaths of 40,000 inmates, including a number of children. In April 1945, as partisan troops were about to liberate Jasenovac, the Ustasha blew up the camp to prevent its discovery. Most of the inmates who had managed to survive to that point died in the blast.

It is difficult to know the actual number of people who died in Jasenovac. Estimates range between 200,000 and more than half a million. The larger number probably includes people who died in the cluster of smaller camps in the vicinity, such as the women's camp at Stara Gradiska. It is estimated that about 25,000 Jewish victims died there, half of them children.

J A S S Y (I A S I)

City in northeastern ROMANIA and formerly the capital of the province of Moldavia. It contained over 100 synagogues and prayer houses on the eve of the HOLOCAUST. Some 35,000 JEWS lived there, which was about 30 percent of the total population.

Jassy and its university were the center of antise-mitic activity in Romania and the birthplace of the IRON GUARD. In November 1940, Ion ANTONESCU came to power, supported by the Iron Guard. The Jews of Jassy suffered arrests, torture, blackmail and robbery. Leaders of the Jewish community bribed the leaders of the Iron Guard, who promised not to harm the Jews further. However, that changed with the (Romanian supported) German invasion of the SOVIET RUSSIA in June 1941. Jews were accused of signaling to Soviet planes and shooting at Romanian and German soldiers. On the eve of 28 June 1941, Romanian soldiers and police ran wild, killing at least 250 Jews in their homes and plundering Jewish property. Almost 5,000 Jews were arrested and forced to board trains made up of sealed cattle wagons. They were kept on the "death trains," without food and water, for up to eight days. During the

Death train from Jassy to Calarasi which has made a stop in Targu-Fromos. Here, a Jew, who has survived this portion of the journey, stands in front of the open doorway of the railroad car which is filled with dead Jews

journey, which was to a LABOR CAMP, about 2,500 people died. Several thousand more Jews were executed in Jassy itself. Estimates of the death toll in the city range from 7,000 to 12,000. The Soviet army entered Jassy in the summer of 1944. There is a monument to the victims of the Holocaust at the Jewish cemetery in Jassy.

J D C

see AMERICAN JEWISH JOINT DISTRIBUTION COMMITTEE.

JEWISH AGENCY FOR PALESTINE

Body established in 1929, which brought together the leadership of Palestinian Jewry with Zionist and Jewish leaders from around the world. It was the representative of the Jews of PALESTINE and of the Zionist movement in international circles. It also was in charge of dealing with the British, who had the mandate to control Palestine at that time. Throughout the HOLOCAUST period, its chairman was David BEN-GURION, and many of its leaders came from the socialist parties in Palestine.

After the Nazi rise to power and before the outbreak of WORLD WAR II, the Jewish Agency for Palestine worked desperately to get Jews out of Europe and into Palestine. It had to face growing opposition from GREAT BRITAIN to Jewish immigration into Palestine. In response, the Jews in Palestine developed ways of working their way around the British blockade by bringing in immigrants "illegally" (see ALIYA BET). The Jewish Agency also worked constantly to alert the nations of the world about the dangers of Nazism. It negotiated deals to bring Jews out of GERMANY and other countries dominated by the Nazis (see BERIHA and HAAVARA AGREEMENT).

Once the war broke out, the Jewish Agency was a natural ally of the countries fighting Nazism. It worked to create a Jewish military group in the Allied armies. This resulted in the mass enlistment of Palestinian Jews in the British army and, in 1944, the JEWISH BRIGADE was formed. At the same time, the Jewish Agency also continued to work against British efforts to prevent Jews from entering Palestine.

The emphasis of the Agency's work during the war was to rescue Jews wherever this was possible.

In 1943, it established an office in Istanbul, Turkey, which maintained contact with Jews in the Balkans and parts of eastern Europe. It helped them financially as much as possible and tried to get them out. Another office was set up in Geneva, SWITZERLAND with similar goals. It passed on money received from the AMERICAN JEWISH JOINT DISTRIBUTION COMMITTEE to help Jews in distress and also organized Jewish RESISTANCE. The Agency persued all leads to the possible rescue of Jews. Some succeeded in saving Jews but others failed. The Jewish Agency made repeated pleas to the Allies to bomb the railroad tracks leading to AUSCHWITZ but these were rejected (see AUSCHWITZ BOMBING).

Another Agency initiative brought Jewish PARACHUTISTS from Palestine into Europe to make contact with the suffering Jews. They tried to raise Jewish morale and to organize resistance behind Nazi lines. The Jewish Agency was limited in its influence and resources. It could not bring about a large-scale rescue, but it did manage to save thousands.

Eliyahu Dobkin, (back) member of the Jewish Agency Executive and head of its immigration department, aboard the S.S. "Yagin" en route to Haifa with a group of Jewish orphans who had been brought out of France to Lisbon with the assistance of the French underground

In 1942, the Jewish Agency made a key decision at a conference in the Biltmore Hotel in New York, called the Biltmore Resolution. It stated that the Jewish Agency was fighting in Palestine not only for a Jewish national home but for a Jewish state. This was achieved three years after the war ended (see ISRAEL, STATE OF).

JEWISH ANTIFASCIST COMMITTEE

see SOVIET JEWISH ANTI-FASCIST COMMITTEE.

JEWISH ARMY

see ARMÉE JUIVE.

JEWISH BRIGADE GROUP

Military unit made up of JEWS from PALESTINE, established in 1944.

When WORLD WAR II broke out, Zionist leaders promised that Jews would support the Allied war effort. They were hoping to fight the Nazis actively and to create conditions for opening up Palestine to Jewish immigration after the war. At first, there

Soldiers of the Jewish Brigade

were discussions about creating a Jewish military division, but the British, who had control over Palestine at the time, did not want to arm Palestine's Jews. Negotiations dragged on into 1941, when the idea of creating a separate Jewish division was finally dropped.

Meanwhile, approximately 35,000 Jewish men and women from Palestine volunteered for the British armed forces. Approximately 3,000 Palestine Jews fought in both FRANCE (May–June 1940) and GREECE (April–June 1941). More than 1,700 were captured by the Nazis and held in PRISONER OF WAR CAMPS.

In mid-1941, the North African battlefront moved toward Palestine. In the summer of 1942, the Jews of Palestine again called for the creation of Jewish combat units. This time, the British agreed to create all-Jewish Palestinian battalions within the British army, but only of equal status as Arab battalions. Since Jewish recruitment far outstripped Arab recruitment in practice, only Jewish battalions were created. New calls for the creation of an independent Jewish division were met with renewed efforts by British military and diplomatic authorities in the Middle East to prevent this from happening. Eventually, opponents in the British government gave in and the Jewish fighting force—now scaled down to a single brigade—was created on 20 September 1944.

The Jewish Brigade was organized like standard British military brigades. Five thousand fighters were in three infantry battalions, an artillery battalion, headquarters and support elements. Most of the officers were British. The Brigade had its own blue and white Zionist flag. All members of the Brigade wore a patch composed of two vertical blue stripes and a yellow Star of David: the BADGE of shame had been turned into a badge of honor!

After intensive training in Egypt, the Brigade moved to the Italian front, where it fought the Germans. It participated in the final Allied drive in northern ITALY.

At the end of the war, the Brigade took part in the Allied occupation of Tarvisio, Italy (near the Yugoslav border). This brought its members into contact with Holocaust survivors and with the early organizers of the BERIHA movement. In July 1945, parts of the Brigade moved to occupation duties in BELGIUM and the NETHERLANDS, although some groups remained in Tarvisio. These groups became involved in secretly transporting Jews who were fleeing eastern Europe to reach Palestine—the "illegal" ALIYA BET. The British broke up the Jewish Brigade in July 1946.

JEWISH FIGHTING ORGANIZATION (ZOB)

("*Zydowska Organizacja Bojowa*")

Jewish armed force set up in the WARSAW GHETTO to form RESISTANCE to the Nazi DEPORTATIONS of Jews to DEATH CAMPS. The ZOB was formed on 28 July 1942. This was during the period of the first, massive wave of deportations to TREBLINKA.

The commanding body of the ZOB was made up of Yitzhak ZUCKERMAN (code-named "Antek"), Josef Kaplan, Zivia LUBETKIN, Shmuel Braslav, and Mordechai TENENBAUM. (Kaplan and Braslav were killed on 3 September 1942.) At first, they were not successful in creating resistance to the Nazis beyond a few isolated acts and they did not gain widespread sympathy with the people, for several reasons. The ghetto residents did not yet understand what the Germans had planned for them. There were also political disputes among the groups represented in the ZOB, which prevented them from cooperating fully. The ZOB activists also failed to gain real help from the Polish UNDERGROUND movement.

After the first wave of deportations, the ZOB attracted many more members and many of the differences between the various political groups were settled. In late 1942, many more organizations joined the ZOB and Mordechai ANIELEWICZ became its commander. In September 1942, authority in the ghetto unofficially passed from the JUDENRAT to the underground groups. The ZOB distributed leaflets throughout the ghetto and prepared the inhabitants for a response to further German actions. They managed to fight off a Nazi round-up operation in mid-January 1943.

The ZOB was instrumental in organizing the resistance carried out in the WARSAW GHETTO UPRISING. With great heroism, the group led the ghetto dwellers during 28 days of fighting before the ghetto's final liquidation. The Germans required 2,000 fully armed troops to defeat the uprising, which was one of the bravest episodes in the HOLOCAUST.

JEWISH LAW

see JEWISH RELIGIOUS LIFE DURING THE HOLOCAUST.

JEWISH RELIGIOUS LIFE DURING THE HOLOCAUST

The goal of the Nazis was to destroy the Jew in body, mind, and spirit. Thus, one important form of Jewish RESISTANCE was the determination on the part of many religious Jews to maintain their religious observances to whatever extent possible.

They went to extraordinary lengths under the most terrible conditions—in the GHETTOS, in hiding, in the underground and even in the DEATH CAMPS. Ingenious new ways had to be though up to observe the everyday rituals, Sabbath and festivals, and events of the Jewish life cycle. Jews risked their lives to save prayer books, ritual objects, and Torah scrolls. Calendars were compiled to guide the Jews in the observance of festivals and fast days. Precious copies of holy books were made. Circumcisions were carried out, although these were the most

Sabbath in the ghetto

risky expressions of religious faith. Women found ways to take ritual baths, and burial societies tried to give corpses proper Jewish burials, until the huge numbers of dead made this an impossibility.

The Jewish holidays were chosen by the Nazis for times of particular cruelty; yet many Jews made su-

perhuman efforts to cling to their observance. The starving population of the STUTTHOF camp was made to stand all day on Yom Kippur in an open field as pots of hot fragrant meat and vegetable stew was offered to them by the Nazis. Some were so feeble that they ate to save their lives. Most resisted the

---

When we arrived, we were put into the blocks at Birkenau. They had previously been horse stables. Among the first things we sought were two ends of candles. Friday night we gathered together on the top tier of our block. There were then about 10 or 12 girls. We lit the candles and began quietly to sing Sabbath songs...we heard choked sobbing from the tiers of bunks all around us. At first we were frightened, then we understood. Jewish women who had been imprisoned months, some of them years, gathered around us, listened to the blessing on the candles. From then on, every Sabbath we lit candles. We had no bread, nothing to eat, but somehow we managed to get the candles.

Rivka Kuper, testimony at
Eichmann trial, from Irving Rosenbaum,
The Holocaust in the Halakhah.

On the day of the Jewish New Year, I went from block to block with a shofar [ram's horn] in my hand. This was very dangerous if the Nazis or the vile kapos should become aware. One thousand four hundred boys who had been condemned to be sent to the crematorium and were locked up in one of the blocks learned that I had a shofar. They began to cry out and plead bitterly that I should enter their block and sound the shofar in their last moments. I decided not to turn them away empty-handed. I began to bargain immediately with the kapos. The truth be written, this decision did not conform to Jewish law, for I well knew that I should not have risked my life for the sake of sounding the shofar. After the sounding of the shofar one boy stood up and cried out, "The rabbi has strengthened

our spirits by telling us that 'even if a sharp sword rest on a man's throat, he should not despair of God's mercy.'"

Rabbi Zvi Hirsch Meisels,
Auschwitz, from Irving Rosenbaum,
The Holocaust in the Halakhah.

Hanukkah was only a few days ahead. I decided that a little Hanukkah lamp would go a long way toward restoring our morale. Two problems had to be overcome: oil had to be "organized," and a place had to be found where the lighted wick would not be seen. We knew, of course, that Jewish law did not compel us to risk our lives for the sake of fulfilling a commandment. But there was an urge in many of us to reveal the spirit of sacrifice implanted in our ancestors throughout the ages. We who were in such great spiritual as well as physical distress felt that a little Hanukkah light would warm our starving souls and inspire us with hope, faith and courage to keep us going through this long, grim and icy winter. I put the stolen oil in the empty half of a shoe-polish tin, took a few threads from my thin blanket and made them into a wick and a little Hanukkah light flickered away slowly, under my bunk. Not only my friends from the "religious" table were there with us but also many others from the room joined us in humming the traditional Hanukkah songs. For a moment nothing else mattered. We were a group of Jewish people, fulfilling our religious duties and dreaming of home and bygone years.

Diary of Simche Unsdorfer, aged 17,
Buchenwald, from Irving Rosenbaum,
The Holocaust in the Halakhah.

entire day to show the Nazis that they would not forsake their sacred day. As evening fell, they said their prayers, repeating over and over again to each other, "Next year in Jerusalem."

Survivor testimonies describe the building of tabernacles, the blowing of a ram's horn on the New Year, the lighting of Hanukkah candles, and the writing of a Scroll of Esther. The dying victims recited the *Shema* ('Hear O Israel the Lord our God, the Lord is One'), the traditional last words of martyrs throughout Jewish history.

Jewish law is strict but distinguished rabbis issued rulings so that a way for observance could be found under ghetto or camp conditions. Rabbi Ephraim Oshry, author of a collection of such rulings, who was in the ghetto in KOVNO, LITHUANIA, permitted electric light to replace Sabbath candles. He allowed people to substitute sweetened tea for unavailable wine at the Passover eve service. A special prayer was prescribed for Jews who had to eat bread on the Passover, referring to the Jewish value of guarding one's life, which took precedence over the commandment not to eat bread during Passover.

J   E   W   S

An ancient people whose origins are described in the Bible (called the Old Testament by Christians). The Jews were the first people to believe in a single God (monotheism). Their religion—Judaism—called for a special way of life and ethics. Their home was in the land of ISRAEL (also known as Canaan and, later, as PALESTINE). They had established communities in other lands as early as the sixth century B.C.E. After they lost their independence in the first century C.E., most Jews lived in the Diaspora—that is, in scattered communities around the world. Wherever they lived they were in the minority. Their special way of life highlighted the fact that they were different from their neighbors. As a result, they were often victims of hostile laws and attacks. This ANTISEMITISM was especially strong in the Christian world. However, Jews were also subject to persecution and discrimination in the Muslim world. Nevertheless, they clung to their way of life, which included a strong sense of community.

Europe was the main center of Jewish life beginning with the Middle Ages. By the nineteenth century, 85 percent of the world's Jews lived in eastern Europe. This was the great center of Jewish religious education and culture. However, toward the end of the nineteenth century, the Jews of eastern Europe faced terrifying persecutions and POGROMS. Millions fled, most of them to the United States.

From the late eighteenth century, there were new ideas about human equality and liberty in western Europe and the United States. This finally brought Jews equal rights as citizens in most of the countries in these regions. With these new rights, many Jews stopped being religious in the traditional way. Some developed modern forms of Judaism, such as Reform and Conservative. Others became "secular" Jews, whose Jewishness was expressed not through religion but largely through their commitment to the Jewish people. At the same time, the focus of antisemitism changed from being religious to being racial (see RACISM). With their new equality, Jews became part of the societies of the countries in which they lived and made significant contributions to all walks of life and culture. However, this did not stop antisemitism. The most fanatical hatred arose in GERMANY, led by Adolf HITLER and the NAZI PARTY. This led to the HOLOCAUST, in which six million Jews were brutally killed. Had Hitler been victorious, he would have killed the entire Jewish people.

The Jews had always longed to return to their own land (Zionism). They hoped they would once again be able to establish an independent nation there. They wished to lead their own lives and make their own decisions, instead of being ruled by other peoples. This goal was fulfilled shortly after the end of the war with the establishment of the State of Israel.

Before the Holocaust, there were seventeen million Jews in the world. By the end of the war there were eleven million. Today, there are still fewer than thirteen million Jews. European Jewish communities are now mostly small in size (see STATISTICS). The two largest communities of Jews are in the United States, with 5.5 million Jews, and Israel, with 4.5 million.

JEWS   IN   THE ALLIED   ARMIES

In WORLD WAR II, Jews in all countries were clearly on the side of the Allies against the Nazi Axis. (This is

JEWS IN THE ALLIED ARMIES

Country	Number
Belgium	7,000
Czechoslovakia	8,000
France	80,000
Greece	13,000
Netherlands	7,000
Palestine	35,000
Poland	140,000
Soviet Union	500,000
United Kingdom	91,000
United States	550,000

1 *Excluding Jews in the Polish and Czech communist armies that were established under Soviet direction in 1943.*
2 *Includes British Commonwealth nations, but not Palestine.*

unlike World War I, when Jews had fought and died for both sides.) Jews joined the army in numbers beyond their percentage in every Allied country. For example, 550,000 American Jews served, out of a total 5.5 million Jews. This is a service rate of 10 percent, even though American Jewry made up less than 3 percent of the total population. The figure for Soviet Jewish war service was 500,000 of a total

Rabbi Alexander Goode (far right) and the three other army chaplains lost with the U.S.S. Dorchester in 1943, on a memorial stamp issued in 1948. They went down with the ship while praying next to each other

Jewish population estimated at 3 million, which is 16 percent. (Soviet Jewry made up less than 1 percent of the total population.)

Thirty-five thousand men and women from PALESTINE served in the British armed forces. Despite the WHITE PAPER OF 1939, the JEWISH AGENCY had a policy of supporting the Allies fully. Of special importance was the creation, in September 1944, of the JEWISH BRIGADE GROUP within the British army. The Brigade also became very important for rescuing Jewish survivors after the war. Jews reached high ranks in all armies, many were killed and many received decorations.

JODL, ALFRED

(1890–1946) Chief of the General Staff of the German Armed Forces, and Adolf HITLER's leading military adviser. He later claimed that he often disagreed with Hitler on the conduct of the war.

In March 1941, Jodl passed on Hitler's directive that the "Jewish-Bolshevist intelligentsia" must be eliminated, since it is the oppressor of the people. Since he did not wish to entrust the job of civilian massacres to the army, he supported the establishment of special units, the EINSATZGRUPPEN, to take charge of the slaughter. Although he later denied it, Jodl's diaries show that he ordered the shooting of hostages and that he was instrumental in planning and carrying out the "FINAL SOLUTION."

Jodl surrendered to the Allies on behalf of GERMANY on 7 May 1945. He was sentenced to death at Nuremberg (see TRIALS OF WAR CRIMINALS) and hanged in 1946. In the 1950s, a German de-Nazification court freed him of guilt, claiming that he "restricted himself to operational questions."

JOINT DISTRIBUTION COMMITTEE

see AMERICAN JEWISH JOINT DISTRIBUTION COMMITTEE.

JOINT RESCUE COMMITTEE

Organization created in PALESTINE by the JEWISH AGENCY in order to help European Jewry during the HOLOCAUST. The committee, also known as the Committee for Jews in Occupied Europe, was set up during WORLD WAR II. In 1939, a four-member Committee for

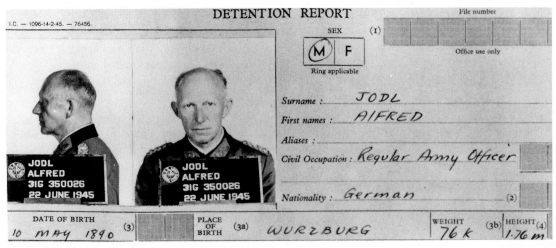

DETENTION REPORT

I.C. — 1096-14-2-45. — 76456.

File number

SEX (1)

(M) F

Ring applicable

Office use only

Surname : JODL

First names : ALFRED

Aliases :

Civil Occupation : Regular Army Officer

Nationality : German (2)

DATE OF BIRTH (3) 10 MAY 1890

PLACE OF BIRTH (3a) WURZBURG

WEIGHT 76 k (3b)

HEIGHT (4) 1.76 m

General Alfred Jodl as he appeared on the detention report, 1945

Polish Jewry was created. It was chaired by Zionist leader Itzhak Gruenbaum, who had been an important figure in Polish Jewry before moving to Palestine. The committee provided modest aid to Polish Jewish REFUGEES.

In November 1942, intelligence reports about the "FINAL SOLUTION" led to more energetic action by the Committee for Polish Jewry. It was changed into the Joint Rescue Committee early in 1943. However, its choices for rescue operations were seriously limited. This was partly because the Allied armies refused to cooperate in rescues, and because the British WHITE PAPER OF 1939 severely limited the immigration of Jews to Palestine.

After the war, the Joint Rescue Committee was actively involved in aiding Jewish DISPLACED PERSONS. It ended its operations in 1947.

JOODSCHERAAD

see NETHERLANDS.

JOYCE, WILLIAM

(1906–1946) British fascist and antisemite. Joyce was active in British fascist (see FASCISM) circles from 1923.

In 1933, Joyce became an early member of the British Union of Fascists under the leadership of Oswald MOSLEY. After functioning as its deputy leader, Joyce left the organization in 1937, mainly because he considered Mosley's anti-Jewish policy

too moderate. He then became a founding member of the National Socialist League. However, this pro-Nazi group failed to gain any popularity in GREAT BRITAIN. Joyce's disappointment grew and he moved to GERMANY in 1939.

From the early months of WORLD WAR II, Joyce delivered strong pro-German, anti-British and anti-Jewish broadcasts to the British people on his radio program, which he always began with the words "Germany calling." The British nicknamed him "Lord Haw-Haw." After Germany's defeat, he was brought back to Great Britain, tried for treason and executed.

JUDENRAT

("Jewish Council")

The German-initiated Jewish Council, which presided over the Jewish population in most GHETTOS.

Shortly after the German invasion of POLAND, Reinhard HEYDRICH issued a secret memorandum to Nazi leaders operating in the conquered Polish territory. He ordered them to instruct Jewish leaders in each major community to establish a Council of Jewish Elders. These councils would be made fully responsible for carrying out future Nazi decrees. Thus, 24 men were appointed from among the local leaders and rabbis of each GHETTO.

For the German authorities, the councils were a tool to use in dominating and ruling the ghettos. The Judenrat represented the Germans in the ghettos, enforced German decrees, and had to do the

The police of the Judenrat in the Warsaw ghetto

Germans' dirty work for them. In many ghettos, they had their own police to enforce order. They also represented the needs of the Jews to the Germans.

The daily tasks of Jewish Councils were like those of a mayor of a city with incredible problems. They had no money, independence, economic opportunity, or freedom of action. Their population was cold, starving, unemployed, and facing a bleak and unknown future. They had to run a local government that could provide food, shelter, heat, medicine, and work to a starving ghetto population.

There were terrible moments that tested the courage and character of Judenrat leaders. The Nazis demanded that they provide the lists of those who would be sent off in DEPORTATIONS. The Judenrat used all strategies of postponement, persuasion, and bribery to avoid doing this, but in the end they had to make the lists. These decisions were handled differently in different places. For example, Mordechai Chaim RUMKOWSKI, chairman of the LÓDZ Judenrat, cooperated. Jacob GENS of VILNA and Moshe MERIN of Sosnowiec also obeyed. Dr. Joseph Parnas, Jewish Council president in LVOV, refused to deliver several thousand Jews for deportation. He was shot. Leaders of the Bilgoraj Council (LUBLIN district) met with the same fate.

The council chairmen of KOVNO and MINSK cooperated with the ghetto UNDERGROUND and RESISTANCE movements, assisting those who fled to the forests.

When the order was finally given to liquidate the entire ghettos, Judenrat leaders faced an even more agonizing dilemma. Rumkowski pleaded with the Jews to go the trains in an orderly fashion. Those who came voluntarily could bring luggage, the others were rounded up by the Jewish police.

The role of the Judenrat has been the subject of much controversy. Their members cooperated with the Germans in the belief that they were helping their community. Especially at first, before the horrors of the "FINAL SOLUTION" were known, they tried to keep the communities together until better days arrived. When the terrible truth was known, it was too late.

Their dilemma was extreme: would handing over some Jews in the ghetto save others, or would it just make it easier for the Germans to destroy all? Immediately after the war, Judenrat members were condemned as collaborators. However, as time passed, people realized that this was true only for some. Many were doing an honest job of trying to preserve Jews and found themselves in a terrible situation.

KALTENBRUNNER, ERNST

(1903–1946) SS leader and head of the REICHSSICHER-HEITSHAUPTAMT (RSHA), the Reich Security Main Office, from January 1943.

Born in AUSTRIA, Kaltenbrunner joined the NAZI PARTY there in 1930. He became a high ranking member of the SS in Austria and was imprisoned on a charge of high treason in 1934. After the ANSCHLUSS (the German takeover of Austria), he became minister for security in the Austrian Nazi government. After Reinhard HEYDRICH was assassinated in May 1942, Kaltenbrunner succeeded him as head of the Reich Security Office. His official title was Chief of the Security Police and SD (the security service of the SS), which included control of the GESTAPO. This gave him authority to order imprisonment and executions in CONCENTRATION CAMPS. He called for the establishment of the camp at MAUTHAUSEN.

Kaltenbrunner was kept fully informed of the murderous activities of the EINSATZGRUPPEN. He had a central role in the killing of Europe's Jews. However, after the war, at the NUREMBERG TRIAL, he insisted on his innocence. He said that he was merely a cog in the machine and that the guilty ones were Heinrich HIMMLER and Heinrich MÜLLER. In fact, Kaltenbrunner had been the overall supervisor of the killing machine. At times he had intervened personally to speed up DEPORTATIONS. This was true in the case of Bulgarian occupied territories in the summer of 1943 and of the Hungarian Jews in 1944. At Nuremberg he was sentenced to death and hanged.

KAPLAN, CHAIM AARON

(1880–1942) Educator; diarist of the WARSAW ghetto. Kaplan was a pioneer of modern Hebrew education in Warsaw, POLAND, and an author of books in Hebrew. He began to keep a personal diary in Hebrew in 1933. When WORLD WAR II broke out, it became a

The time may come when these words will be published...material for the chronicle of our agony. This obligates those who are writing impressions to record every event, every small detail which might shed light upon the darkness of foul, depraved souls. It is beyond my capabilities to record every event in organized form. But even events recorded in reportorial style are of historical value. They reflect a truth—not a dry, embalmed truth but a living, active truth proclaiming before the world: "Behold, there is no pain like unto mine." Listen and you will hear.

From Chaim Kaplan's Diary
20 February 1940

chronicle of the suffering of Warsaw Jewry.

The first weeks of the war were so terrible in Warsaw, with the bombardment, chaos, death and the beginning of the persecution of the Jews, that Kaplan wished for the arrival of Adolf HITLER's army—it seemed then that nothing could be worse. "We have turned into animals," he wrote, but by the end of November 1939, under Nazi rule, he noted, "it is hard to watch the death of a community." At the same time, he praised the Jews' spiritual struggle as the community refused to be trodden on like animals and demonstrated "a will to live and a hunger to learn." Kaplan struggled to keep his schools running until the Jews were isolated in ghettos and all schools were closed. He carefully concentrated on observing the day-to-day fate of the Warsaw Jewry, with its tragedies, problems and even its humor. In March 1940, he asked, "We are so debased and depressed, is it possible we can sink even lower?" By 1942, the diary rose to its climax of agony as rumors circulated that Jewish communities in Eastern Europe were no longer in existence. An escapee from CHELMNO brought confirmation of the horrors of the DEATH CAMPS.

Kaplan strongly condemned the JUDENRAT appointed by the German authorities over the Warsaw ghetto, and its head Adam CZERNIAKOW. He described how many of the ghetto's Jews were rounded up in July 1942. He commented, "We have reached the extremity. Death is precious when it is swift. Have we truly sinned more than any other nation? Have we transgressed more than any generation?" When his friends advised him to stop writing, since no one would be left to receive his DIARIES, he wrote, "I must record. Perhaps I am the only one engaged in this work." Kaplan and his wife were deported to their deaths in TREBLINKA in 1942.

Kaplan's diary was discovered after the war, hidden in a kerosene can on a farm near Warsaw. It is one of the most valuable and vivid sources for life in Warsaw between 1939 and 1942. An English translation by Abraham I. Katsch was published as *The Warsaw Diary of Chaim A. Kaplan* in New York (1965).

K A P O

Term used for a prisoner in a Nazi CONCENTRATION CAMP appointed by the SS as a labor foreman over other prisoners. The word was probably derived from the Italian *capo* ("boss").

Kapos held the power of life and death over the prisoners in their group and were generally characterized by sadistic cruelty. They inflicted ruthless humiliations on those in their command to break their spirits. The Kapo was often recruited from among known German criminals. In those camps where all the prisoners were Jewish, there were also Jewish Kapos.

The Kapos acted as the instrument of the SS in supervising workers at hard labor and ensuring that their daily work quota was fulfilled. In return, the Kapos received special privileges from their superiors. Some of them showed a humane side, but most were brutal and even whipped them with iron rods until they were almost dead. Many Kapos were put on trial after the war, charged with war crimes and crimes against humanity.

K A R A I T E S

Sect that broke away from Judaism in the eighth century. The total number of Karaites world-wide during the 1930s is estimated at 12,000, with the largest concentration in the SOVIET UNION. Some also lived in FRANCE.

With the passing of the NUREMBERG LAWS in 1935, Karaites living in Berlin became concerned that they would be mistaken for Jews. They approached the Nazi authorities with the claim that they were not of Jewish racial origin, and therefore the laws of racial definition did not apply to them. In October 1939, the Karaites were officially informed that they were not considered to be Jews. Racially, they were considered to be blood relatives of the Turks and Tatars, a conclusion supposedly based on racial examination.

When the EINSATZGRUPPEN mobile killing units arrived in the Soviet Union along with the regular German army in 1941, they requested clarification on how to treat Karaites. Unusually, the Nazis referred the question to Jewish scholars in the ghettos. In an effort to spare the Karaites, they declared them to be of non-Jewish origin. The original ruling was upheld and the Karaites were spared. Apparently before this clarification reached all the killing units, 200 Karaites were killed at BABI YAR.

In a few instances Karaites informed the Germans about Jews presenting forged Karaite documents; in other cases, Karaites helped to save Jews. In 1944, over 500 Karaites were found to be serving in the SS units, and Heinrich HIMMLER recommended that they be allowed to continue serving.

K A R S K I ,   J A N

(1914–) Undercover name for Jan Kozielewski, a non-Jewish junior Polish Foreign Ministry official who brought news of the HOLOCAUST to the west. When the war broke out, he fought in the Polish army and was captured by the Soviets. He escaped from captivity and returned to POLAND. He served as a courier in the Polish Home Army, and traveled several times between Poland and GREAT BRITAIN, bringing news of the situation in his native land and especially of the plight of the Jews.

Karski visited the WARSAW GHETTO twice and met

with Jewish leaders there. He presented their demands to the west: bring pressure on GERMANY to stop its policy of mass murder, conduct revenge bombings of German cities, make public announcements accusing the Germans, and reveal the facts of the Holocaust to the world. He was also smuggled into the CONCENTRATION CAMP at Izbica-Lubelska (which at the time he believed was BELZEC). He brought the news of the starvation and slaughter of Jews there to the attention of the Polish GOVERNMENT-IN-EXILE and later to United States President Franklin D. ROOSEVELT, and other western leaders. When it became clear that Karski's identity was known to the Germans, he could not return to Poland. He then worked for the Polish government-in-exile. In 1944, he published the account of his secret visit to Poland, *Story of a Secret State*.

When the war ended, Karski stayed in the United States, where he became a professor of government at Georgetown University. Karski's efforts in bringing news of the Holocaust to the west were recognized by YAD VASHEM. He received the "RIGHTEOUS AMONG THE NATIONS" award and honorary Israeli citizenship.

KASZTNER AFFAIR

see KASZTNER, YISRAEL (REZSÖ RUDOLF).

KASZTNER, YISRAEL (REZSÖ RUDOLF)

(1906–1957) Hungarian Zionist activist. Kasztner was a journalist who became vice-chairman of the RELIEF AND RESCUE COMMITTEE OF BUDAPEST, which worked to save JEWS from the Nazis. The Committee had received information that there was a possibility to negotiate with the Nazis to save many Hungarian Jews. The Nazis said they would free one million Jews from HUNGARY and neighboring countries in exchange for 10,000 trucks and large quantities of other supplies. Kasztner got Adolf EICHMANN to release some 1,700 Jews as a token of proof that the offer was serious. The Rescue Committee had the painful task of compiling the list of people to make up the "transport" of those to be saved. It included 500 Zionist pioneers trying to move to PALESTINE, some leading rabbis, members of different Jewish

religious communities as well as Kasztner's immediate family. The train, made up of cattle cars, left BUDAPEST on 30 June 1944, and eventually reached neutral SWITZERLAND. Kasztner made several trips to GERMANY and Switzerland to continue negotiations and to get the money to pay for the rescue efforts from the AMERICAN JEWISH JOINT DISTRIBUTION COMMITTEE (JDC) and the JEWISH AGENCY. He was also able to convince Eichmann to deport an additional 20,000 Hungarian Jews to STUTTHOF in AUSTRIA instead of the DEATH CAMP at AUSCHWITZ. Most of them survived. Kasztner moved to Palestine in 1947 and joined the editorial staff of the Hungarian-language newspaper published in Tel Aviv.

In 1953, Malkiel Gruenwald, an elderly Jew of Hungarian origin, published a pamphlet accusing Kasztner of collaborating with the Nazis in the murder of Hungarian Jewry. He also condemned Kasztner for giving evidence in the TRIALS OF WAR CRIMINALS at Nuremberg in support of Kurt Becher, a former SS officer who had helped in organizing the rescue. Gruenwald was sued for libel. The judge declared that "Kasztner had sold his soul to the devil" and found for Gruenwald. However, an appeal was

Yisrael (Rudolf) Kasztner

made to the Supreme Court which totally cleared Kasztner and found Gruenwald guilty of vicious libel. Even before the decision was published, Kasztner was shot down in the street by an extreme rightist youth. He became the first victim of political assassination committed by a Jew in Israel.

K A T Y N

Site near Smolensk, Russia, where the Soviets massacred Polish military officers taken prisoner after the Soviet invasion of eastern POLAND in 1939. Some 15,000 Polish officers were shot in the spring of 1940. Five thousand died at Katyn and another 10,000 at Starobielsk and Ostachkov, also in Russia. Several hundred Jews were among the victims, including the chief rabbi of the Polish army and Dr. Henryk Strasman, an important activist in the Zionist movement.

The mass graves of these victims were only discovered after the German invasion of SOVIET RUSSIA. At that time, German authorities appointed a group of doctors from various countries under Nazi control to investigate the crime. All evidence pointed to the Soviet Secret Police. However, the Soviets denied the charges and accused the Germans of executing the officers. Only with the end of communism did Russian authorities admit that the Soviets were indeed responsible.

A monument, which also recognizes the Jewish victims, marks the site.

KATZMANN, FRITZ

(1906–1957) ss and police official, involved in the murder of the Jews of Eastern Galicia (UKRAINE).

Katzmann joined the SS in 1930. He rose to the rank of SS major general and lieutenant general of the police. He served from November 1939 to the end of 1943 as SS and police leader in the GENERAL-GOUVERNEMENT, first of the Radom district, and then of Galicia Most of the JEWS of Eastern Galicia were murdered under his direct command. Jews were brutally rounded up in the GHETTOS and executed immediately, or sent to DEATH CAMPS (mainly BELZEC and SOBIBÓR). Katzmann was responsible for the liquidation of the LVOV ghetto in June 1943.

In 1944, Katzmann was transferred to DANZIG. After the German defeat, he went into hiding under another name and nothing is known of him after that except the date of his death.

KATZNELSON, YITZHAK

(1886–1944) Poet and dramatist writing in both Yiddish and Hebrew. Before WORLD WAR II, he lived and taught in LÓDZ, POLAND.

From almost the start of the war, Katznelson and his family were confined to the WARSAW ghetto, where he joined the Zionist underground. He was in the ghetto until May 1943, when he was deported to Vittel CONCENTRATION CAMP in FRANCE. Then, in April 1944, Katznelson was deported again, this time to AUSCHWITZ, where he and his only surviving son were murdered.

While living in the Warsaw ghetto, Katznelson kept a journal and wrote hundreds of poems, of which the most famous is "The Song of the Slaughtered Jewish People" (see box). He began writing this poem while he was still in Warsaw and completed it in Vittel. The poem is a chilling account of

Yitzhak Katznelson

The birds and fishes knew—all of us knew;
The Gentiles all around us—they knew too.
We would be murdered; each of us was
doomed.
No reason given; nothing to be done.
The order had been issued, stark and plain;
"Slaughter the Jewish people!"—child and
man.

From Yitzak Katzenelson's poem The Song
of the Slaughtered Jewish People" (1944).

Wilhelm Keitel

the reality and tragedy of the time. It recorded what
was known by Jews about the HOLOCAUST and their
responses—especially their fear of accepting the
finality of their situation.

K E I T E L   O R D E R

see NIGHT AND FOG.

K E I T E L ,   W I L H E L M

(1882–1946) Field-marshal and chief of staff of the
German Armed Forces from 1938 to 1945.

Keitel was close to the NAZI PARTY as early as 1934.
He had great admiration for Adolf HITLER as a person
and as a military strategist. He rose rapidly through
the ranks of the army and was promoted to the
newly created post of chief of staff of the WEHRMACHT
in 1938. Keitel was in part responsible for the cor-
ruption of ethics in the German army, which allowed it to serve the criminal aims of the Nazi
regime. Keitel signed a series of orders for the
shooting of hostages and the execution of civilians
and prisoners of war in the Nazi-occupied territories. Keitel signed the "NIGHT AND FOG" decree (also
known as the Keitel Order), which ordered the
army to put down resistance movements in western
Europe. He issued the KOMMISSARBEFEHL (Commissar
Decree), which authorized the execution of Russian
Communist Party political officials. He also signed
the document for the unconditional surrender of

GERMANY in May 1945. After the war, at the NUREMBERG
TRIAL, he represented the army's High Command,
which was on trial as a criminal organization. He
was sentenced to death and hanged.

K I E L C E

City in south central POLAND. In 1939, its Jewish population was approximately 25,000, which was about
35 percent of the total population. It was occupied
by the Germans on 4 September 1939. Jews were
immediately subjected to various antisemitic laws. A
GHETTO was established on 31 March 1941, and a JU-
DENRAT appointed. Its first leader was deported to
AUSCHWITZ when he refused to follow German orders. Conditions in the ghetto were extremely difficult and many died from disease and starvation. In
1941, some 4,000 people died during a typhus epidemic. Several thousand Jews from Vienna were deported to the Kielce ghetto in 1941. The ghetto was
liquidated in August 1942, when 20,000 Jews were
deported to their deaths at TREBLINKA. About 2,000
Jews were held in a FORCED LABOR camp in the city. All
attempts to organize a RESISTANCE movement in the
camp failed. In 1942, half the prisoners were sent to
other work camps. In August 1944, the last prison-

I was almost 11 when the war was officially over and my parents rented an apartment in Kielce. The apartment had five rooms and there was some kind of kitchen and bathroom. Five Jewish families lived in the apartment, a room for each family, and to us that was a great luxury.

My father had to make a living. So he would travel into another town [by train] to buy and sell. This train station was just a block away from our house and I always walked him to the train. This one day I said, "Please don't take this train" and I started crying and begging. He did not take the train. I don't know why he listened to me, an 11-year-old. Ten Jews were killed on the train. Poles went from car to car and whenever they saw a Jew either they killed him outright or threw him off the train while the train was moving.

Everybody in the building except for that one apartment was Polish. My father made friends with one of the men on the floor below us and he was best friends with him. They went to the movies. They called each other "comrade." My father was so happy he had a friend. All his time during the war he didn't have anybody. The man would come to our room every night, and they played cards and my mother would serve tea.

We moved to Bytom and within days of leaving Kielce there was the Kielce pogrom. Everybody in our apartment was killed. All four families. There was a boy and girl who lived in one of the rooms. She was 16 and he was 17. They got married right after the war, in that room. They were just the two of them. They didn't have anybody. The Russians caught the ringleaders of the pogrom and one of them, if not the main ringleader, was the man who drank tea in our apartment every night—my father's comrade, my father's best friend. He was hanged by the Russians.

From the testimony of Bernice Graudens Fishman, Gratz College Oral History Archives

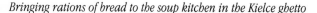

Bringing rations of bread to the soup kitchen in the Kielce ghetto

ers of the Kielce camps were sent to Auschwitz.

After the war, some Jewish survivors returned to the community from SOVIET RUSSIA. However, on 4 July 1946, a Polish mob attacked the building of the Jewish committee, shooting, stoning, and smashing to death every Jew they could lay their hands on. These mobs had been stirred up by hateful rumors that Jews had kidnapped Christian children to use their blood. Among the 42 men, women, and children killed there, were 7 who could not be identified. One of them bore an Auschwitz number on his arm. This attack caused 100,000 Jews—half the survivors left in Poland—to leave the country. There is still a debate about who started this pogrom, and whether the communist authorities were involved. A new investigation by the Polish government opened in 1995. There is a memorial plaque at the site of the tragedy and a monument in the Jewish cemetery.

K   I   E   V

Capital city of the UKRAINE, a republic of SOVIET RUSSIA. Kiev was a major center of Jewish culture before WORLD WAR II. At that time, 160,000 Jews lived in Kiev, which was about 25 percent of the total population.

The German army occupied Kiev on 19 September 1941. About 100,000 Jews managed to flee eastward before the arrival of Nazi troops. Those who did not flee were doomed.

Immediately following the Nazi occupation of the city, a number of German army buildings were blown up by the Soviet Secret Police. For revenge, the Germans decided to kill all the Jews of Kiev. A massacre took place on 28–29 September at BABI YAR. In the following months, thousands more Jews—as well as GYPSIES, SOVIET PRISONERS OF WAR, and PARTISANS—were shot at Babi Yar. According to Soviet estimates, over 100,000 people—mostly Jews—were shot there. The exact number will probably never be known.

Many of the Jews not brought to Babi Yar were sent to the FORCED LABOR camp in Syretsk, just outside Kiev. The Jews left in the city, including the mentally handicapped, were continuously terrorized. On 29 March 1942, the Nazis took 365 Jewish patients from a psychiatric hospital and killed them in mobile gas vans (see GAS CHAMBERS, GAS VANS, AND

German soldiers marching through the streets of Kiev

CREMATORIA) in the Kirillow forest.

The Soviet army liberated Kiev on 6 November 1943. Besides those who had escaped to eastern Russia, only a few hundred Kiev Jews in hiding survived the Holocaust.

KINDERTRANSPORT

("Children's Transport")

The transporting of Jewish children from GERMANY and other Nazi-occupied countries during the prewar years. Thousands of children who were allowed to leave the European mainland were sent without their parents to places of temporary or permanent refuge. A main place of shelter for 10,000 Jewish children was GREAT BRITAIN. The events of KRISTALLNACHT in November 1938, the round-up of 30,000 JEWS by the Nazis and the pressure of local groups, all helped move the British government to admit the children.

The term *Kindertransport* was also used for Nazi deportations of Jewish children during the war to DEATH CAMPS. It referred to the convoys of trucks or trains that were solely made up of Jewish children seized in Nazi round-ups and sent to their deaths. These children were almost all scheduled for immediate gassing, since they were not considered capable of working. Adam CZERNIAKÓW, the chairman of the WARSAW GHETTO JUDENRAT (Jewish Council), committed suicide in despair when he realized that he was not capable of preventing the ghetto orphans from being deported to TREBLINKA.

KOCH, KARL OTTO and ILSE

Karl Otto (1897–1945) and Ilse (1906–1967). Nazi camp commandant and his wife and collaborator. Karl Koch joined the NAZI PARTY in 1930 and the SS in 1931. After serving in a number of senior positions in various CONCENTRATION CAMPS, he was made commander of BUCHENWALD in 1937. His wife, Ilse, accompanied him there with the rank of SS supervisor.

The couple soon became notorious, not only among the prisoners but even among the camp's staff. Karl Koch was cruel and corrupt while Ilse was a sadist. She was fond of horses, and was often seen galloping through the camp and beating passing prisoners with her whip.

In September 1941, Koch was transferred to MAJDANEK. His first responsibility was to oversee this camp's transformation from a LABOR CAMP for Soviet prisoners of war into a DEATH CAMP, where an estimated 350,000 people eventually died. There the couple amassed a ghoulish collection of shrunken heads and tattoos. Ilse often chose which tattoos would be placed on her victims before they were killed and then tanned the skin and made it into lamp shades, gloves and book jackets.

Karl Koch was removed from his post in 1942, following a mass escape from the camp. Although he was later acquitted of negligence, he was considered too sadistic even by many senior SS officials and was transferred to the postal security service. He was soon charged with embezzlement and "other charges"—probably from his time in Buchenwald and Majdanek. He was sentenced to death by the SS Supreme Court and executed. Ilse Koch was acquitted of involvement in her husband's crimes. She was arrested by the Americans in 1945 and sentenced to life imprisonment in 1947. Two years later, she was suddenly pardoned and released, but as a result of public outrage, she was immediately rearrested and given another life sentence. She committed suicide in prison in 1967.

KOMMISSARBEFEHL

("Commissar Decree")

Order which was issued to the WEHRMACHT (the German army) shortly before its attack on the SOVIET UNION (22 June 1941). The decree defined the way in which the campaign was to take place. It described the responsibilities of the Wehrmacht and the SS. It

Karl Otto Koch

Ilse Koch

ordered that all civilian commissars (Soviet government department heads) suspected of sabotage were to be shot. If there was no evidence of sabotage, they were to be handed over to the SD, which would result in the same fate. All military commissars were to be shot on the spot by the German soldiers.

The written text of the decree was finished only after much negotiation, in which army generals took part. Since the decree was so secret, German soldiers were informed of it only verbally. The decree shows that the German army was deeply involved in the murders committed by the Nazi regime.

KORCZAK, JANUSZ

(Pen name of Henryk Goldszmit; 1879–1942) Polish Jewish doctor, educator, and author of plays and classic books for children. He devoted his life to the care of orphans and ultimately went with them to his death.

Korczak was born in WARSAW. He completed his medical studies and became involved with the running of institutions for Jewish and non-Jewish children. He wrote educational books, such as *How to Love a Child* and *The Child's Right to Respect*, and children's books. His *King Matthew the First* became a classic that was translated into many languages and was made into a play.

In 1912, he was appointed director of a new Jewish orphanage in Warsaw. He introduced many new approaches as he defended the rights of children. He encouraged them to govern themselves and participate in running the orphanage. He later founded and directed another orphanage for non-Jewish children. He was a popular radio broadcaster under the name of "Old Doc."

In the 1930s, rising ANTISEMITISM in POLAND led him to consider moving to PALESTINE and living in a kibbutz. He went there twice, in 1934 and 1936, and met with former orphanage children. However, he decided that his place was with his children in Warsaw. When GERMANY occupied Poland in 1939, Korczak, who had many non-Jewish friends, might have escaped, but he decided to remain with his orphans. He spent several months in jail because he refused to wear the yellow BADGE. He was finally released and moved into the Warsaw GHETTO together

> *In the message he gave graduates leaving one of his orphanages, Janusz Korczak wrote: "We have not given you God because you must search for him and find him within yourself.... We do give you one thing, however. We give you a longing for a better life, based on truth and justice, which you are destined to build for yourself."*

with the 200 children of his orphanage. The diary he kept there is a tragic testimony to the fight of an aging and ailing man desperately trying to keep his children safe and secure. On 5 August 1942, during mass DEPORTATIONS from the ghetto, the Germans came to take the children away. Korczak refused to stay behind. He marched to the railway station at the head of the column of frightened children, holding their hands or carrying them and telling them they were going out to the countryside. When one child remembered she had left her doll behind, Korczak reassured her, "Never mind, they will send it on to us." The German authorities made a last attempt to convince Korczak to let the children go without him. They feared the bad publicity that the death of such a respected doctor and educator could cause. He refused and boarded the train,

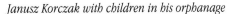

Janusz Korczak with children in his orphanage

KORCZAK'S LAST WALK

The Doctor goes down with the children without forgetting to take the green flag—the flag of the Orphanage.

According to eye-witnesses, the children were dressed in their holiday clothes, as though they were going for a trip or for a holiday in the country.

As though in a dream, the children's procession marches forth with song and flag. The tired old Doctor, dressed in the uniform of a Polish officer, whose heart is breaking from unbearable pain, slowly leads it. The night marish ghetto street is dusty, parched and burning. The children are suffering and sweating. They want to drink. They are overcome by heat and terror. Now and again they raise their voices and we can hear the weak, childish choir. They lose the tune and the choir ceases. The Doctor moves his legs with great difficulty, bending beneath his load and his troubles—but then straightens himself in a mighty effort to hold out to the end. Above him flutters the green flag of the Orphanage.

(Published by World Ha-Shomer ha-Tzair)

which left for the DEATH CAMP at TREBLINKA. Nothing more was heard of the doctor or the children.

KOVNO (Kaunas)

City in LITHUANIA. Kovno became the national capital after Lithuania declared its independence in 1918. It was one of the most important centers of Jewish culture in eastern Europe.

The lives of Lithuania's JEWS were changed when SOVIET RUSSIA gained control of the country in June 1940. The Soviet government nationalized private businesses. A high percentage of these businesses were Jewish. Jewish political and social groups were banned, and Jewish schools were closed. Although Soviet law granted the Jews equal citizenship, the damage to the Jewish community was devastating.

WORLD WAR II struck Kovno on 24 June 1941, two days after GERMANY invaded Soviet Russia. As the Soviets retreated and the Germans approached, law and order collapsed. Bands of Lithuanian nationalists started a POGROM that, within a few days, left sev-

Belongings of deportees left behind in Kovno

The main gate to the Kovno ghetto and a view of the bridge to Slobodka (a painting by Esther Lurie)

eral thousand Jews brutally murdered. The nationalists blamed the Jews for Soviet rule. They were also encouraged by German antisemitic PROPAGANDA. The German EINSATZGRUPPEN (mobile killing squads) that accompanied the German army organized local people to help with roundups of Jews. Most Jews were marched to Fort Seven, a nearby fortress, and shot. By mid-July 1941, the Einsatzgruppen and their Lithuanian COLLABORATORS had killed 7,800 Jews.

Under German control, Kovno's Jews faced anti-Jewish laws. This included orders to wear a yellow BADGE on their front and back. They were also forced to turn over all their possessions, from valuables to electrical appliances and pets. On 11 July 1941, Kovno's 30,000 Jews were ordered to move into Slobodka, a suburb of Kovno, then home to only 8,000 people. The Jews had to choose a Jewish Council (JUDENRAT) and form a Jewish police force. They elected the highly respected Dr. Elkhonan Elkes to lead the council. On 15 August, Slobodka became the fenced-in Kovno GHETTO.

Three days later, the Germans told the Jewish Council to gather 500 of the ghetto's educated professionals for office work. The volunteers, believing they would have "easy" jobs, were marched to Fort Four and killed. For two more months, hundreds of others were given various false reasons for assembling. All were taken to Fort Four and shot.

By 28 October 1941, the ghetto population was down to 26,000. The Germans ordered all residents to gather at a field on the ghetto's edge. There the GESTAPO commander "selected" 10,000 residents with a wave of his hand: "to the left; to the right." Soon it become clear that those sent "to the right" were selected to die. Nine thousand two hundred Jews, almost half of them CHILDREN, were taken to FORT NINE and shot.

This temporarily ended the mass killings. The 17,000 ghetto residents who had been spared were drafted as FORCED LABOR for the German war machine. They built an airfield nearby, and served the Germans' personal needs, in laundries, as tailors, and in other crafts. The Jewish Council, aided by the ghetto police, supervised their work.

The Kovno ghetto became a Gestapo-run concentration camp in September 1943. Several thousand residents were sent to smaller LABOR CAMPS outside the city. On 27 March 1944, some 1,800 preteen children and elderly were seized and killed. In July, more than 4,000 were sent to concentration camps in Germany. Elkhonan Elkes died in DACHAU in October 1944. Many ghetto inhabitants managed to avoid deportation by using hiding places, including underground bunkers. Dozens of others slipped away into the surrounding forests to join the small bands of RESISTANCE fighters. Some parents persuaded sympathetic Lithuanian families to hide their children so that at least they could survive.

During the ghetto's final days in July 1944, the Germans used firebombs to force out those in hiding. They killed 2,000 in the effort and destroyed the ghetto. Fewer than 100 Kovno Jews lived to see the arrival of the Soviet army on 1 August. At the war's end, only some 3,000 Kovno Jews remained alive. Most were liberated by Allied forces in German concentration camps.

KOVNER, ABBA

(1918–1988) Hebrew poet and PARTISAN leader. Kovner was born in Sevastopol, Russia. He attended Hebrew high school in VILNA and was a member of Ha-Shomer ha-Tza'ir, a left-wing Zionist youth

> *Jewish youth, do not believe those who are trying to deceive you. Out of 80,000 Jews of Vilna only 12,000 are left. Where are our own brethren from other ghettos? Those taken through the gate of the ghetto will never return. All the Gestapo roads lead to Ponary [see entry], and Ponary means death. Let us not be led like sheep to the slaughter. True, we are weak and helpless, but the only response to the murders is self-defense. Brethren, it is better to die fighting like free men than to live at the mercy of the murderers. To defend oneself to the last breath.*

Abba Kovner, 31 December 1941

group. He lived in the Vilna ghetto after the Germans invaded LITHUANIA. He was one of the chief organizers of Jewish RESISTANCE there. His call to fight the Germans inspired young Jews throughout eastern Europe (see box).

Kovner understood Adolf HITLER's plan to kill all the Jews of Europe. It took him 18 months to con-

Partisans in Vilna. Abba Kovner is standing in the center

vince the Jews of Vilna that armed resistance was the proper response. When Yitzhak WITTENBERG, the commander of the United Partisan Organization (FPO), was betrayed, Kovner became its commander. After the uprising in Vilna in September 1943, he escaped to the nearby Rudninkai forest, where he was a partisan leader. When the Soviet army pushed back the Germans, he led a group that was committed to acts of revenge on the Germans and their collaborators. After the war, he became an organizer of BERIHA, planning mass escapes of Jewish survivors from eastern Europe to freedom in the west, which later led them to PALESTINE. He settled on a kibbutz in Israel with his wife Vitka Kempner, who had been a partner in the underground movement. He became one of ISRAEL's most influential writers.

K R A K Ó W

POLAND's third largest city. JEWS had been living there since the Middle Ages. In the years before WORLD WAR II, Jewish cultural life flourished in Kraków, although there was ANTISEMITISM.

When the German army occupied the city on 6 September 1939, 60,000 Jews lived in Kraków. Nazi persecution of Jewish residents began immediately. EINSATZGRUPPEN (mobile killing units) began random shootings of Jews. The city was chosen as the Nazi capital of occupied Poland, and therefore all anti-Jewish decrees for Poland's Jews were issued there. Many German military and political personnel lived in Kraków. Thus, the Nazis had a special commitment to make the city "Judenrein" (rid of Jews). As Hans FRANK, Nazi governor of occupied-Poland stated: "We must take care that the German city of Kraków shall be entirely cleansed of its Jewish character."

In the early days of German occupation, the Jews of Kraków were subject to constant acts of Nazi terror. In October 1939, Jewish males between the ages of 14 and 60 were drafted for FORCED LABOR. In November, Jews were ordered to wear a yellow BADGE. In December, the Germans raided Jewish property in the city and burned down several synagogues. In the process, 180 Jews were tortured to death.

A JUDENRAT (Jewish Council) was established on 28 November 1939, headed by Dr. Marek Bieberstein.

Like other Jewish Councils, the Kraków Judenrat had the dilemma of trying to make life as tolerable for Jews as possible, while at the same time obeying German orders. The GESTAPO arrested Bieberstein in the summer of 1940. Dr. Artur Rosenzweig was appointed to be the new Judenrat chairman.

On 1 May 1940, a decree was issued which made several of the city's main squares and boulevards off limits to Jews. Expulsions also began in May. Within one year, 40,000 Jews were expelled to nearby communities.

A GHETTO was established in Kraków in March 1941. The 20,000 Jews left in the city had to move into the ghetto area, which was enclosed by a wall and barbed-wire fence. Thousands of Jews from neighboring towns were also forced to live in the ghetto, where conditions were crowded and unsanitary. Some Jews worked outside the ghetto walls in German factories. The Judenrat ran a number of aid organizations in order to relieve the harsh conditions.

DEPORTATIONS from the Kraków ghetto began in March 1942. On 28 May, the Germans began deporting Jews to the DEATH CAMP at BELZEC. All were gassed on arrival. During this AKTION 6,000 Jews were deported to Belzec. Judenrat Chairman Artur Rosenzweig was ordered to produce lists of Jews for deportation. He refused to cooperate and was shot. The Germans then disbanded the Judenrat and formed another Jewish organization (Kommissariat) in its place.

The Nazis' goal of destroying Kraków's Jews met with some opposition. From the early days of the ghetto, Zionist YOUTH MOVEMENTS established UNDERGROUND cells to carry out RESISTANCE activities. In October 1942, the JEWISH FIGHTING ORGANIZATION (Zydowska Organizacja Bojowa; ZOB)—similar to the one in WARSAW—was established.

The ZOB had a single aim: armed struggle against the Germans. Due to the ghetto's small area, the ZOB decided to carry out armed resistance in the non-Jewish section of Kraków. They attacked sites commonly visited by German soldiers. During one attack, 11 German army officers were killed at a cafe. The ZOB also called for Jewish PARTISAN activity—fighting the Nazis in the forests near Kraków. This was not successful, however, due to the antisemitism of local Polish partisans who were also fighting the Germans.

Jews made to clean the street in Kraków

Despite these acts of resistance, the deportations continued. In October 1942, the Nazis ordered the Kommissariat to compile a list of 4,000 Jews for another deportation. Again, the leaders refused to comply, and again the Germans launched another Aktion. On 27–28 October, the Nazis rounded up 7,000 Jews and deported them to Belzec and AUSCHWITZ. During this Aktion, the old age home and orphanage were destroyed.

Following this deportation, the Germans divided Kraków ghetto into two sections. Section A contained Jews with work permits, and Section B contained those without. On 13 March 1943, the 2,000 residents of Section A were deported to the PLASZÓW FORCED LABOR camp, where only a few hundred survived. A German factory owner, Oskar SCHINDLER, was able to rescue 900 Jews from Kraków by bringing them to his own industrial compound. Schindler spared these Jews from the harsh conditions at Plaszów.

The Germans then liquidated Section B, by deporting 2,300 Jews to Auschwitz, where they were all gassed. The remaining 700 Jews were shot on the spot.

When soldiers of the Soviet army liberated the city on 18 January 1945, there were no more Jews left in Kraków.

KRAMER, JOSEF

(1906–1945) Commandant at AUSCHWITZ-II, (Birkenau), and BERGEN-BELSEN. Kramer joined the NAZI PARTY in 1931. He became a member of the SS and worked in several CONCENTRATION CAMPS. He started as a guard in DACHAU in 1934, but quickly moved up through the ranks in several camps, including SACHSENHAUSEN and MAUTHAUSEN.

For most of the war, from mid-1941 to mid-1944, Kramer was the commandant at the NATZWEILER camp. In May 1944, he was moved to Auschwitz, where he was responsible for the GAS CHAMBERS at Birkenau. He supervised the gassing of hundreds of thousands of Hungarian Jews and others. He was transferred to Bergen-Belsen on 1 December 1944. Belsen had no gas chambers, but, many thousands of prisoners died there under his cruel administration from deliberate starvation and neglect. He was known as the "Beast of Belsen."

Kramer was arrested when the British liberated Bergen-Belsen. A British military court at Luneburg, Germany, sentenced him to death for his war crimes on 12 November 1945 and he was executed.

KRISTALLNACHT

("Night of Broken Glass")

Pogrom (attack on Jews) carried out by the Nazis on 9–10 November 1938. Its name comes from the thousands of windows that the Nazis smashed. It is also called the November Pogrom.

On 7 November 1938, Herschel GRYNSZPAN, a young Jewish refugee, shot Ernst vom Rath, a German Embassy official, in Paris. Vom Rath died of his wounds two days later. A severe POGROM was then launched throughout GERMANY and occupied-AUSTRIA.

Nazi leaders had gathered that evening in Munich to celebrate the anniversary of the abortive Beer Hall Putsch of 1923. They were told by Josef GOEBBELS that Adolf HITLER had decided that if anti-Jewish riots spread "spontaneously" throughout the Reich, they were not to be discouraged. The NAZI PARTY was not to appear as the architect of the riots but was to organize and execute them. The riots spread with lightning speed.

The Nazis themselves estimated that 267 synagogues were burned and 76 of them completely destroyed (in fact the number was much higher). In addition, 815 Jewish shops and 29 warehouses were destroyed and 171 homes burned down. Ninety-one Jews were killed.

The SA sent its brigades to burn synagogues and other Jewish-owned property. Heinrich HIMMLER, chief of the SS and police, ordered his forces not to stop the destruction but only to prevent large-scale looting. At the same time, he ordered the arrest of some 30,000 Jews who were sent to the CONCENTRA-TION CAMPS of SACHSENHAUSEN, BUCHENWALD, and DACHAU. They were treated with cruelty and hundreds died. Moreover, the Jews had to pay a fine of 1 billion marks.

The process of ARYANIZATION of the German economy was intensified. Those arrested were released in 1939 and allowed to leave Germany. For this privilege they had to give up all their property and assets.

Kristallnacht is considered to mark the beginning of the end of European Jewry. It sent shock waves through the western world, and alerted many for the first time to the evils of the Nazi regime. It led some countries in western Europe to admit more refugees, especially children. Since the end of WORLD WAR II, the day is remembered in synagogues and churches all over Germany.

Kristallnacht exhibit at Beth Shalom Holocaust Education Center near Nottingham, England

Burning of a synagogue on Kristallnacht, Siegen, Germany

In Dusseldorf, Rabbi Eschelbacher had just re-turned home at midnight on 9 November when the telephone rang: "A voice, trembling with horror, shouted—'Rabbi, they're breaking up the synagogue hall and smashing everything to bits, they're beating the men, we can hear it from here.' It was Mrs. Blumenthal, who lived next door (to the hall). I was just about to go there, but almost at that very moment there was a vio-lent banging at my own door. I switched off the light and looked outside. The square in front of the house was black with SA men. The next mo-ment they were upstairs, pushing in the front door of the flat. The staircase swarmed with men, of all ranks. They rushed in on us shout-ing: 'Revenge for Paris! (the murder of Ernst vom Rath). Down with the Jews!' They pulled mallets out of their pouches and in a moment splintered glass flew from window-panes and mirrors, and splintered wood from the furniture. The gang came up to me with clenched fists, one of them got hold of me and ordered me down-stairs. I felt certain I would be beaten to death. I went into the bedroom, put down my watch, wallet and keys and took leave of Berta.

"Downstairs the street was full of SA men. Counting those in the house there must have been between fifty and sixty altogether. The shout met me: 'Give us a sermon!' I began to speak of the death of Vom Rath, saying that his murder was more of a misfortune for us than for the German people, that we were in no way guilty for his death.... On the corner, in the Stromstrasse, the street was covered with books that had been thrown out of the window, to-gether with papers, documents and letters. The ruins of my typewriter were there also.... I myself was gripped by an SA man and hurled across the street against the house.... The party Kreisleiter [official] said to me: 'You are under arrest.'"

Rabbi Eschelbacher was then escorted to Dus-seldorf police headquarters by SA men who sang in unison "Revenge for Paris! Down with the Jews!" Passers-by joined in the chorus.

From *Pogrom, 10 November 1938*
by Lionel Kochan

KRUPP WORKS

Large German industrial firm. During WORLD WAR II, the Krupp Works was GERMANY's major producer of tanks and armaments. Its factories used CONCENTRA-TION CAMP inmates as FORCED LABORERS.

When Adolf HITLER came to power in 1933, he promised leading industrialists that he would rearm Germany. Gustav Krupp, head of the Krupp Works, supported Hitler and became an officer in the Adolf Hitler Fund, which made financial contributions to the NAZI PARTY and the SS. Gustav's son, Alfred, was influential in the firm even before officially taking over from his aging father in 1943. He joined the Nazi Party in 1936.

At the beginning of World War II, the Krupp Works formed a huge industry with branches rang-ing from armaments manufacture to mining. Its plants were located throughout Germany, among

other places, in Essen, Kiel, and Magdeburg. The firm prospered during the war and expanded be-tween 1939 and 1943. Part of this growth came from absorbing industries in German-occupied regions. Some Krupp factories were established in eastern Europe, near concentration camps. This allowed them to use prisoners as forced laborers. Many Jew-ish and Polish prisoners and SOVIET PRISONERS OF WAR served as forced laborers. The great majority died from cruel treatment and inhuman conditions.

At the end of the war, the elder Krupp was arrested as a major war criminal. However, he was 74 years of age he was found unfit to stand trial because of ill health. Alfred Krupp was arrested as a war criminal and was tried in 1948. He was sentenced to 12 years in prison and his property was taken away. This ver-dict was later overturned. He was released in 1951 and allowed to take control of the Krupp factories until the firm became a public corporation in 1968.

KULTURBUND DEUTSCHER JUDEN

("Cultural Association of German Jews")

Jewish SELF-HELP organization that was established in BERLIN on 6 July 1933, as a response to the exclusion of JEWS from German cultural life.

On 26 April 1935, the GESTAPO ordered the Kulturbund Deutscher Juden to change its name to *Jüdischer Kulturbund, Berlin* ("Jewish Cultural Association of Berlin") and one day later the branch in Berlin and other local branches established a nationwide *Reichsverband der Jüdischer Kulturbünde* ("Reich Union of Jewish Cultural Associations"). By organizing a broad range of cultural activities, the Kulturbund, under the leadership of the musician Kurt Singer, offered work to Jewish actors, musicians, and artists who had lost their jobs in 1933. At the same time, it provided the German Jewish public with cultural offerings, in which the audience and artists were all Jewish. The only non-Jews attending the performances were GESTAPO agents and members of the Chamber for Arts and Culture, which tightly controlled the Kulturbund.

The Kulturbund opened in Berlin on 1 October 1933, with a performance of *Nathan the Wise*, an 18th-century play by the German playwright Gotthold Ephraim Lessing, calling for religious tolerance. Other activities included operas, concerts, art

Dr. Kurt Singer directing Handel's "Israel in Egypt" at a concert by Jewish musicians given for Jews in Berlin, 1937

exhibits, and lectures. In early 1938, there were 76 branches in 100 towns with more than 50,000 members and 1,700 artists. Although German Jews had been forced into a cultural ghetto, the program was designed to present them with cultural expressions in universal terms.

The Kulturbund was allowed to exist until 11 September 1941. Most of its artists were killed in the Nazi DEATH CAMPS.

L A B O R   C A M P S

Camps established by the SS during WORLD WAR II in order to exploit slave labor in the territories occupied by the Germans. After the war broke out in 1939, much of the German work force was drafted into the army. Since the Nazis needed more workers, they forced thousands of Polish and SOVIET PRISONERS OF WAR and laborers to work in terrible conditions for very little pay.

The Jewish population in the Nazi-occupied areas was abused this way to an even greater degree. In autumn 1939, a German decree stated that FORCED LABOR would be required for JEWS. The Nazis often raided the GHETTOS, rounded up Jews, and forced them to do hard labor in the local area.

From 1940, closed LABOR CAMPS were established for Jews. These included JANÓWSKA in LVOV, PONIATOWA near LUBLIN, and PLASZÓW in KRAKÓW. Prisoners usually worked in the manufacture of armaments or textiles. Jews were brought from the VILNA ghetto to the Klooga camp, built in ESTONIA in 1943, to work mainly in producing cement and bricks for Nazi fortifications.

Conditions in all of these CAMPS were intolerable. The work was backbreaking, and the food and sanitary conditions were shocking. The guards, usually recruited from the local population, such as Ukrainians and Lithuanians, were often brutal. Exhausted prisoners were routinely beaten and shot. Many were sent to DEATH CAMPS.

L A M B E R T ,   R A Y M O N D -
R A O U L

(1894–1943) Head of the UNION GÉNÉRALE DES ISRAÉLITES DE FRANCE (UGIF), the Jewish council set up by the VICHY government to run the affairs of the Jewish community in FRANCE.

The UGIF was established on the order of the Germans. Its purpose was to force all the Jewish organizations in France to combine into one group. The Germans felt that this grouping would make it easier for them to gain control of the large sums of money that belonged to all the Jewish organizations in France. Lambert became leader of the UGIF in the unoccupied zone of France. He worked to create the maximum amount of independence possible for Jewish organizations under the circumstances.

In 1943, Lambert protested against the Nazis' confiscation of Jewish property. As a result, he and his family were deported to AUSCHWITZ, where they were gassed on their arrival.

L A T I N   A M E R I C A

Southern half of the continent of America. At the time of Adolf HITLER's rise to power in 1933, there were 20 independent countries in Latin America. The countries differed from one another in most aspects—size population, economy, and importance. They also had varying proportions of immigration from Europe in the nineteenth and twentieth centuries. Some nations (ARGENTINA, Uruguay, Chile and the southern part of Brazil) were really Euro-American countries, where there were many Jewish communities. Mexico and Cuba, also had considerable numbers of JEWS.

Early in 1935, James G. McDonald, the LEAGUE OF NATIONS' High Commissioner for REFUGEES from GERMANY, attempted to find homes in Latin America for several thousand people who had escaped from Germany. They were waiting in refugee camps in Europe, where they were not allowed to remain. He found animosity and resistance to his attempt in Brazil and Argentina, tolerance and good will in Uruguay and Chile, extreme welcome in Ecuador, and mixed attitudes in other countries. Three years later, at the EVIAN CONFERENCE, Latin American nations were asked to help solve the refugee problem. The Dominican Republic was the only country that expressed willingness to receive refugees.

The Dominican Republic declared that it was ready to settle gradually not less than 100,000 refugees. This amount was far beyond what it could actually accommodate. Following this declaration, the AMERICAN JEWISH JOINT DISTRIBUTION COMMITTEE financed the establishment of the Dominican Republic Settlement Association. It started its work when WORLD WAR II had already begun and managed to establish one small colony—Sosua—with 444 Jewish refugees.

The eighth International American Conference met in Lima in December 1938. KRISTALLNACHT had occurred just a month earlier and had shocked public opinion throughout the world. However, it did not lead conference representatives to agree to adopt a recommendation in favor of immigration. Bolivia was the only nation to suggest such a move, but with no results. Yet, what governments officially rejected, lower government employees—especially consuls—carried out.

Tens of thousands of immigration, transit and tourist visas were issued—usually sold—by many Latin American representatives in Germany, AUSTRIA, FRANCE, and other countries. In 1939 and 1940, the forging of documents became a source of wealth for many people, including officials. It became a challenge to governments to be able to tell if a visa issued in their name was real or fake. Some cases became well known—like that of the S.S. SAINT LOUIS, whose 906 passengers were turned back from the port of Havana, Cuba. Other countries especially Bolivia—allowed the refugees to enter their territories.

In January 1942, all Latin American nations except Argentina and Chile, declared war on, or severed ties with, Germany. It then was much more difficult for them to intervene on behalf of Jews in Europe. Chile followed suit in January 1943, while Argentina did so reluctantly as late as January 1944.

In spite of all the official restrictions, it is believed that some 112,000 Jewish immigrants managed to enter Latin America during the Nazi years. They established new communities in some countries, such as Ecuador and Bolivia, where there were no Jews before 1933. They enriched existing large communities in Argentina, Brazil, Chile, and Uruguay, and they diversified Jewish life in other communities like Mexico and Venezuela.

L A T V I A

Country on the Baltic Sea. On the eve of the HOLOCAUST, some 92,000 Jews lived there. By the end of the war, 72,000 of them had died.

The country was taken over by SOVIET RUSSIA in the spring of 1940, in keeping with the secret NAZI-SOVIET PACT. Under Soviet rule, all Jewish community institutions were shut down. Many Jewish leaders and wealthy members of the community were arrested and deported to FORCED LABOR camps inside Russia.

The Germans invaded Russia in June 1941, but even before they arrived in Latvia, the torment of the Jews was begun by Latvian nationalists. In RIGA, the capital, a synagogue to which Jews had fled for protection was set on fire, with heavy loss of life. The German EINSATZGRUPPEN carried out the first mass murder in Libau (Liepaja) at the end of July, when 4,000 Jews were gunned down. On 25 October 1941, the Germans forced 32,000 Riga Jews into two GHETTOS. Only 37 days later, the ghetto's liquidation was begun. On the night of 29–30 November, some 15,000 Jews were shot in the Rumbuli forest. On 8 December, another 12,000 were shot in Bikernietzi forest. Both of these sites, not far from Riga, became permanent places of execution for the Jews left in the Riga ghetto. Ghettos were also established in Libau and Daugavpils (Dvinsk) and most of the inhabitants of these towns met the same fate as the Jews of Riga.

Some 15,000 Jews from GERMANY and elsewhere were also deported to Latvia. In November 1941, thousands of Jews from BERLIN and other German towns were sent to the Riga ghetto and took the place of those who had been killed. They were employed in slave labor, although in some cases the new arrivals were taken directly from the trains to killing grounds. By August 1943, all Jews had been murdered or deported to LABOR CAMPS.

Latvia was the site of several CONCENTRATION CAMPS. The largest two were Kaiserwald and Salaspils, near Riga. In the summer of 1944, just before the arrival of Soviet forces, the survivors were sent to STUTTHOF.

Many Latvians helped the Germans. Volunteers

served in the DEATH CAMPS and took part in putting down the WARSAW GHETTO UPRISING.

LAVAL, PIERRE

(1883–1945) Prime Minister of FRANCE under the VICHY government during WORLD WAR II, and a leading collaborator with the Nazis. Laval was a leading figure in right-wing French parties before the war and a sly politician. He served in various important government positions, including as prime minister and foreign minister.

Laval's contacts with Italian and German dictators in the mid-1930s convinced him that FASCISM was the best form of government and that democracy was out-of-date.

Following the Nazi occupation of the northern half of France in June 1940, Laval became chief aide to Marshal Philippe PÉTAIN, head of the Vichy government (which collaborated with the Nazis). Pétain's fear that Laval would attempt to take power from him, led to Laval's dismissal from the government in December 1940. However, the Nazi authorities insisted that he be brought back. In the spring of 1942, Laval returned to the Vichy government as prime minister.

Laval believed in peace at any price. To that end, he adopted a policy of total cooperation with the Axis powers. He even declared, "I desire the victory

Latvians welcoming German soldiers arriving in Riga, June 1941

of GERMANY." Parliamentary democracy was abolished under Laval, and Vichy was turned into a totalitarian government.

Laval was easily persuaded that the non-French JEWS from both the occupied and the unoccupied zones of France should be deported. His government cooperated fully in carrying out the DEPORTATIONS. It was Laval's suggestion that children under 16 be included in the deportations from the unoccupied zone.

After the liberation of France, Laval tried to escape to SPAIN. He was caught and handed over to the American authorities in AUSTRIA, who returned him to France to face trial. He was found guilty of treason against the French republic and of collaboration with the enemy. He was executed in PARIS in November 1945.

LEAGUE OF NATIONS

International organization founded after World War I.

The Allied powers (who had won the war) made treaties with most eastern and Central European countries, which required them to protect their minorities. This was very important for the JEWS in those countries. The League of Nations was in charge of making sure that the countries honored these treaties. Jewish organizations turned to the League a number of times when the rights of Jews were threatened or violated, especially in POLAND and ROMANIA. The League was also active with REFUGEE problems. It appointed a High Commission for Refugees in 1933 to supervise the program of moving Jews out of GERMANY. However, the first high commissioner, James G. McDonald (later the first United States ambassador to ISRAEL), was extremely discouraged at the inability of his office to protect people. He resigned in protest at the end of 1935.

Generally, the League was unable to prevent Nazi persecution of Jews, other minorities and political opponents, but there were some minor exceptions. After receiving petitions from Jewish organizations, the League was able to delay the application of the NUREMBERG LAWS in Upper Silesia (part of Poland that had been combined with Germany). It also arranged for the orderly emigration of the Jews from the Saar and DANZIG areas before Germany annexed them.

During its short existence, the League of Nations failed to fulfill its declared aim of "establishing world peace and the promotion of cooperation among states." The organization that took its place was the United Nations. It was established in 1945.

LEBENSBORN ("Well of Life")

A Nazi program designed to encourage the bearing of "racially valuable" children.

The SS leader Heinrich HIMMLER was obsessed with racial purity (see RACISM). He wanted to see a Nazi empire populated by the "Aryan" elite, the "race" he considered most valuable. He was disturbed that the German birthrate had consistently dropped after 1919 and felt that this harmed Nazi plans to dominate Europe, both economically and militarily. Himmler's solution was to create a program of re-education about sexual and child-bearing practices.

The Lebensborn society was begun in December 1935. Its early aims were to give financial assistance to SS families with large numbers of children and to provide maternity facilities to expectant mothers (including the unmarried) of "valuable" racial stock.

The program failed to produce enough "Aryan" children, so it was gradually expanded. A new policy was to encourage adoptions of suitable children. This was followed by the decision to seize the children of "racially valuable" parents in the THIRD REICH and the Nazi-occupied territories. Most of these children were taken from eastern and southeastern Europe. The majority were war-orphans, but some were taken from their parents. There is very little information available about the numbers involved.

LEBENSRAUM ("Living Space")

Adolf HITLER's notion that GERMANY was too small to contain the "ARYAN master race," and that it should, therefore, expand eastward into the SOVIET UNION. There, the local population would be enslaved or, in the case of Jews and intellectuals, exterminated. In his book MEIN KAMPF, Hitler wrote: "For Germany, the only possibility of carrying out a healthy territorial policy lies in the acquisition of new land in Europe itself. It can be obtained, by and large, only at the expense of Russia."

In fact, Hitler had reinterpreted a much older German belief, dating from before World War I, that since there was not enough potential farm land in Germany to fill the needs of a growing population, the country should build up a colonial empire in Africa. After World War I, the term was used by nationalists who demanded the return of Germany's former lands in Europe and overseas.

LE CHAMBON SUR LIGNON

Small town in southern FRANCE with a mainly Protestant population, where thousands of JEWS were saved during the Nazi occupation of France. The local pastor, Andre Trocmé, took the initiative and inspired the townspeople to follow their conscience and save Jewish lives—even at the risk of their own. Resistance began when the schoolchildren, inspired by their elders, refused to give the Nazi salute to the French flag. When the local prefect visited the school, he received a document from the students stating their intention to hide Jews whenever possible. When he protested that "foreign Jews are not our brothers," Trocmé responded, " We do not know what Jews are. We know only people." The whole village and surrounding area participated in sheltering Jews—in homes, farmhouses, and institutions—even during searches. Indeed, the protective mood was so infectious that even some of the VICHY police cooperated.

The situation became more dangerous, however, after the summer of 1942, when the Germans occupied southern France and the GESTAPO, the political police organization of the Nazi regime, became involved. Trocmé's brother was arrested on charges

> *In almost every interview I had with anyone from Chambon, there came a moment when they looked in my eyes and said "How can you call us 'good'? We were just doing what had to be done. Who else could help them? And what has all this to do with goodness? Things had to be done, that's all, and we happened to be there to do them. You must understand that it was the most natural thing in the world to help these people."*
>
> Philip Hallie, an American professor of ethics, in *Lest Innocent Blood Be Shed* (New York, 1979).

of hiding Jews and was deported to MAJDANEK, where he was put to death. A leader of Trocmé's Reformed Church asked him to halt his activities, but Trocmé refused and was supported by his own religious council. Hundreds of Jews reached Le Chambon. Some were hidden for lengthy periods, others for a shorter time, until they could move on to safe havens—often to be smuggled across the Swiss border. In the summer of 1943, Trocmé learned that he was wanted by the Nazis and was forced into hiding for almost a year. Nevertheless, the work was carried on by his wife and the rest of the town. In all, it is estimated that between 3,000 and 5,000 Jews of all ages were sheltered by the people of Le Chambon. This model story of ethical behavior has been told by Philip Hallie, an American professor of ethics, in *Lest Innocent Blood Be Shed* (New York, 1979).

LEMKIN, RAPHAEL

(1901–1959) Jurist who coined the term "GENOCIDE" in 1943. Lemkin was born in eastern Europe but escaped to the U.S. after the outbreak of WORLD WAR II.

Lemkin defined genocide as the deliberate extermination of an ethnic, religious or national group. He also suggested that it could be a gradual process aimed at the destruction of the foundations of the life of such a group with the intention of annihilating it. Lemkin's term was used as the basis for the United Nations Genocide Convention adopted by the General Assembly in December 1948.

LEVI, PRIMO

(1919–1987) Italian author who wrote many books on his experience as a prisoner in AUSCHWITZ. Born in Turin in 1919, he was trained as a chemist. He was involved with an anti-FASCIST group, and was arrested when the Germans took over ITALY in December 1943. He was sent to Auschwitz in February 1944, along with other Italian Jews, and was liberated in January 1945.

As early as 1947, he published his first account of CONCENTRATION CAMP life in a book entitled *If This be a Man; Survival in Auschwitz*. The book was at first ignored, but later became a classic. Levi continued to work as a chemist through 1973 and then retired to devote all his time to writing.

Primo Levi

Auschwitz and the human condition after Auschwitz is a constant theme of Levi's work. He wrote *The Reawakening*, which describes his journey back to Italy from Auschwitz. His work, *The Periodic Table*, describes his postwar work with German supervisors at Auschwitz-Buna. In 1986, he

> You who live safe
> In your warm houses,
> You who find, returning in the evening,
> Hot food and friendly faces:
> Consider if this is a man
> Who works in the mud
> Who does not know peace
> Who fights for a scrap of bread
> Who dies because of a yes or a no.
> Consider if this is a woman,
> Without hair and without name
> With no more strength to remember,
> Her eyes empty and her womb cold
> Like a frog in winter.
>
> From *Survival in Auschwitz*

published his greatest book, *The Drowned and the Saved*, which deeply and sorrowfully probes the human condition.

No writer has written as darkly of this period. In sharp, unemotional prose, he describes the full extent of the horror and the evil.

At first, he had hoped that his books would help heal the world. As he grew older, he grew more disappointed and depressed. His death, when he fell down the stairwell of his home, is widely regarded as a suicide, born out of despair.

L E Y , R O B E R T

(1890–1945) Nazi leader. Ley was a World War I veteran and member of the Nazi Party from 1924. He was crudely antisemitic and was frequently jailed for his violent behavior. In 1932, he became Adolf HITLER's chief of staff and from that time was in the Reich leadership. His power in the THIRD REICH came from being head of the German Labor Front, the huge labor organization set up to replace the banned Trades Unions in May 1933. The Labor Front had divisions called "Strength through Joy" and "Beauty of Labor" meant to give mass appeal to

Robert Ley

Nazism. During the war, Ley also became Reich Commissioner for Public Housing. He was captured by the Americans in 1945, and committed suicide in his cell in Nuremberg, GERMANY.

American soldiers with survivors in Buchenwald

L I B E R A T I O N

As the Allies reconquered the territories that had been occupied by the Germans, they came to the sites of the many Nazi DEATH CAMPS and CONCENTRATION CAMPS. In some places, the Germans had tried to destroy all evidence of the camp. In others, only the buildings remained, as the inmates had been moved elsewhere, often on DEATH MARCHES. In many camps, deathly thin survivors were found. They were sick, starving, and surrounded by scenes of indescribable horror.

The liberation of CAMPS began in eastern Europe. In late July 1944, the Soviet army reached the camp at MAJDANEK. They also discovered the often camouflaged sites of other Nazi death camps in POLAND. The Soviet authorities did not always reveal to the rest of the world all that they had uncovered.

In the west, British and American soldiers did not reach the major concentration camps in GERMANY until the spring of 1945. The soldiers were unprepared for the dreadful sites they encountered. They found

DACHAU IS FREED

Angry troops storm through horror camp: 32,000 set free

DACHAU, Monday.—Thirty-two thousand people in the infamous prison camp here were freed to-day by the 42nd and 45th Divisions.

The infantry, riding tanks, bulldozers, "Long Toms"—anything on wheels—came in from the north west and surprised the S.S. guards.

54-HOUR WEEK FOR BUILDERS

No Sunday work

The working week in the building and civil engineering industries is to be reduced throughout the country from May 14 to a maximum of 54 hours.

General permission for Sunday work in London will also cease from that date.

Scores of guards were taken prisoner and dozens were slain as the U.S. troops, enraged by the horrible sights they saw, ranged through the camp, using machine-guns, pistols and rifles.

Polish, French and Russian prisoners seized S.S. weapons and joined their liberators in revenge.

There were 50 railway trucks crammed with bodies.

From officials it was learned that Stalin's son, the Austrian Chancellor Schuschnigg and his wife, Prince Leopold, Pastor Niemoeller, and the Prince of Lichtenstein were removed to a new hideout a few days ago.

Evening Standard newspaper, London, 30 April 1945

not only corpses, but tens of thousands of dying people. There was a high death rate in the weeks after liberation. The Allied soldiers made great efforts to help the survivors. Photos and movies of the newly liberated camps caused shame and anger in the countries when they were located. In some places, groups of local Germans were taken by the Allied troops to the camps so that they could see for themselves what had happened. After the liberation, most of the non-Jewish prisoners returned to their homes. However, the majority of the Jews no longer had homes. They remained in camps in or near the sites of the concentration camps. As DISPLACED PERSONS they stayed where they were, usually for years, before eventually finding a permanent home. The great majority settled in the State of ISRAEL.

L I B Y A

Country in northern Africa. From 1912, it was ruled by ITALY. In 1922, the local government started taking orders from the new Fascist (see FASCISM AND FASCIST MOVEMENTS) leadership in ROME, headed by Benito MUSSOLINI. The governor, General Italo Balbo, was quite tolerant toward the 27,000 JEWS living in Libya. However, from 1938, he had to follow antisemitic orders coming from Italy. Balbo asked Mussolini to ease some of the restrictions relating to the Jews,

Still dressed in prison uniforms, prisoners cheer madly as U.S. troops approach Dachau

I was in the 81st Armored Medical Battalion, which was a part of the 11th Armored division. At this time it was assigned to Patton's Third Army. We were traveling through Germany and were told that there was a camp which had been operated by the Nazis. It contained mostly Jewish inmates but also political inmates of many races and from many countries. This was the camp called MAUTHAUSEN.

I was in the lead jeep at the time. As commanding officer of the medical battalion, I led the contingent that was sent to Mauthausen to investigate. When we got there the gates were closed. But we saw above the gates at least a dozen inmates who looked in rather decent condition. They were all Spanish political prisoners. They jumped down and opened the gates.

As we drove into the compound, the first shocking sight that greeted us was a pyramid of bodies of roughly 6,000 humans. All of them were completely naked, most of them obviously starved to death.

As we traveled around the camp, other smaller piles of bodies were present. It was obvious that these bodies were corpses that the enemy had been unable to destroy completely by burning or burying. They had made much use of the gas chambers, of which personally I saw two. The horrors around the camp were one of the most incredible sights I had ever seen, despite the fact that we had very, very recently been in combat.

We were equipped to handle only battle casualties. But help arrived rather quickly. In fact, too much help. Because food was rushed in, I'm sure that many of the survivors died from overfeeding. They had been starved for so long, that they were unable to handle it. There must have been a couple of thousand still living, many of whom died from malnutrition and disease that first week we remained in camp.

Orders were received from headquarters of the Third Army that the bodies would be buried in individual graves. This was signed by General Patton. He wanted to make sure that the Austrians or Germans could never say that they had known nothing. The orders indicated that the work was to be done by the local citizens.

From the testimony of Dr. Nino de Prophetis,
Gratz College Holocaust Oral History Archive

but Mussolini refused.

Balbo died in 1940 and was succeeded by General Ettore Baspicao. Baspicao was not only more antisemitic than his predecessor, but also more antise-

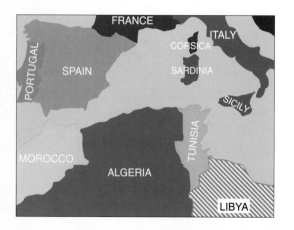

mitic than his superiors in Rome. Libya became the most oppressive country for Jews under Italian rule.

The situation grew even worse for Libyan Jews in 1941. At that time, the German army came to the aid of the Italians, who were being defeated by the British army in North Africa. In March 1941, the Germans and Italians outlawed all Jewish organizations in Libya. In April, the local Fascists organized riots and attacked Jews. Jewish merchants had to mark their stores with the Star of David. Jews had to post a sign on their houses, saying "Jew." All Jews working in public offices were fired and the government established more and more financial restrictions.

In spring 1941, the Italian government started to deport Jews to CONCENTRATION CAMPS and FORCED LABOR CAMPS in Libya, notably in Bukbuk, Siddi Azaz, and Giado, which was the biggest and held 2,600 Jews.

Soldiers of the Jewish Brigade in Libya

The prisoners worked mainly at digging ditches in the nearby mountains. German officers were involved in administering the camp. At least 562 Jews died at Giado. About 1,400 Jews were imprisoned in five other camps, and some were murdered.

Jews who were French and Tunisian citizens were deported to TUNISIA, and shared the fate of other Tunisian Jews. Those who were British subjects, numbering approximately 300, were deported to Italy early in 1942 and imprisoned in camps. In 1944, they were deported to the main concentration camps in Europe.

About 1,000 Libyan Jews were murdered by the Nazis and their allies. Those who survived were liberated by the British army in January 1943.

LICHTENBERG, BERNHARD

(1875–1943) German Catholic anti-Nazi. He was ordained a priest in 1899. During World War I, he served as a military chaplain. After the war, he became a well-known member of the Berlin city council, representing the Center Party. In 1938, he was appointed Provost of St. Hedwig's cathedral in Berlin.

In August 1941, Provost Lichtenberg sent a letter of protest to the senior physician of the German Ministry of the Interior. This was on behalf of a dis-

tressed mother whose son had been cremated in a mental hospital as part of the EUTHANASIA PROGRAM. Later that month, he offered a public prayer for the "Jews and wretched prisoners in the CONCENTRATION CAMPS" and publicly denounced an anti-Jewish PROPAGANDA pamphlet that had been widely distributed. Lichtenberg was reported to the GESTAPO, put on trial, and sentenced to two years' imprisonment for improper use of the pulpit and violating the treason law. He died in captivity on the way to DACHAU concentration camp. In 1996, the Vatican started the process for his beatification—being declared a saint.

L I D I C E

Czech mining village in Bohemia, 10 miles northwest of PRAGUE. In September 1941, Reinhard HEYDRICH was appointed as acting governor of BOHEMIA AND MORAVIA. His main task was to smash the groups of freedom fighters that struggled against the German occupation.

The Czech government-in-exile in London decided to drop paratroop partisans inside occupied CZECHOSLOVAKIA to act against the Germans. In October 1941, a number of such teams were parachuted inside Czechoslovakia. On 27 May 1942, when Heydrich drove to Prague, two partisans, assisted by a

Bodies of inhabitants of the Czech village of Lidice shot by Germans in the retaliation for murder of Reinhard Heydrich

partisan group from the vicinity, attacked his car with hand grenades. Heydrich died of his wounds on 4 June. The Germans then declared a state of emergency and arrested 3,180 Czechs; 1,344 were executed. Three weeks later, the assassins were captured and killed. In order to prevent future sabotage activities, Josef Bohne, Security Police Chief of Prague, decided to take revenge. This action was called "Operation Lidice." On 10 June 1942, all of Lidice's 192 male inhabitants were massacred as were 71 women. One hundred and ninety-eight women were deported to RAVENSBRÜCK concentration camp and ninety-eight children were deported to so-called "German Education Institutes." The village was leveled completely. In addition, 252 friends and relatives of Lidice residents were murdered at MAUTHAUSEN concentration camp. The official excuse for this barbaric action was that the assassins were helped by a partisan group from the vicinity, an accusation that was not true. After the war, Lidice became a symbol for the cruelty of the German occupation.

LITERATURE OF THE HOLOCAUST

Events as large and complex as the Holocaust usually require a long period of time to be understood. They must be seen in some perspective before they can become the subject of literature. An exception happened in POLAND, where a number of literary works appeared during the Holocaust. Best known is a Yiddish poem, "Song of the Murdered Jewish People," written by Yitzhak KATZNELSON who later died in AUSCHWITZ. As time went by, survivors began to publish DIARIES and memoirs. One of the first works of Holocaust fiction to come out after the end of the war was *The Wall*, by the American writer John Hersey, published in 1950. It was inspired by the story of Emanuel RINGELBLUM, historian of the WARSAW GHETTO. Hersey reconstructed in an accurate and moving way the history and everyday life of the Warsaw ghetto.

Among the most influential of the survivors to write about the Holocaust was Elie WIESEL. His

SOME MAJOR WORKS OF LITERATURE ON THE HOLOCAUST

Aharon Appelfeld, In the Wilderness (1963). A collection of stories by a Holocaust survivor, translated into English from their original Hebrew. Through allegory and symbolism, the stories relate to the Holocaust as an always existing fact and not only as an event of the past.

Romain Gary, The Dance of Genghis Cohen (1969). A tale of a Jewish comedian killed in the Holocaust who returns to haunt his executioner.

Günter Grass, The Tin Drum (1965). A German novel in the form of a fictional autobiography. Oskar, a mad midget in Danzig, recalls the Nazi regime and mocks its development.

Rolf Hochhuth, The Deputy (1964). A play in German that condemns Pope Pius XII for not having spoken up against Adolf Hitler's treatment of the Jews. Many Catholics objected when this controversial drama appeared.

Jerzy Kosinski, The Painted Bird (1966). A novel based on Kosinski's horrifying experiences in Poland during the Holocaust. A refugee child wanders between persecution and threat, witnessing the gruesome human atrocities.

Primo Levi, If This is a Man (1959). A story based on Levi's experiences in the Auschwitz concentration camp, to which he had been deported in 1944. Originally written in Italian, the work describes the camp and its atrocities.

Arthur Miller, Incident at Vichy (1966). An American play that tells of the Nazi occupation of Vichy France, through a series of arrests of Frenchmen, some of them Jews.

Nelly Sachs, O the Chimneys (1967). A Nobel Prize winning collection of poetry, translated into English from German. The poems reflect the poet's reactions to the "Final Solution," through metaphors and images of dust, smoke, flight and metamorphosis.

André Schwarz-Bart, Last of the Just (1961). A French novel based on the traditional Jewish legend of the "Thirty-Six Hidden Saints" who exist in every generation. It portrays the martyrs of the Jews of Europe from the 12th century to the Holocaust.

Jean-François Steiner, Treblinka (1967). The story of the Treblinka death camp, based on a collection of written and oral testimonies. Steiner's goal is to understand the initial cowardly helplessness of the camp's inmates and the daringly heroic resistance that followed.

William Styron, Sophie's Choice (1979). An American novel that tells the story of Sophie, a young survivor of the Auschwitz-Birkenau death camp, as it is revealed to a young and naive American. The novel studies issues of evil, guilt, and violence.

Leon Uris, Mila 18 (1960). An American novel telling of the Jews of the Warsaw ghetto and their rise in revolt against the Nazis.

Peter Weiss, The Investigation (1966). A play based on the trial of the Nazi war criminals of Auschwitz at Frankfurt, Germany. Originally in German, the work made use of the documents of the Frankfurt trial.

Elie Wiesel, Night (1960). Wiesel's first novel. The book is based on his tragic experiences in the Auschwitz and Buchenwald concentration camps.

powerful works, inspired by his experiences, were written in French and translated into English. The authors of works that appeared in Europe were often survivors. They wrote for a readers who had themselves experienced the events of WORLD WAR II. Two outstanding poets of the Holocaust who wrote in German emerged in Europe: Nelly Sachs, who received a Nobel prize for her poem "O the Chimneys," and Paul Celan, a survivor from Romania whose best known poem is "Fugue of Death." Both Celan and the great Italian Holocaust writer Primo LEVI were so haunted by their Holocaust experiences that they committed suicide.

Many works appeared in Hebrew and Yiddish in Israel, some of them by survivors (Avraham Sutzkever, Abba KOVNER, Aharon Appelfeld). Others were by younger writers (such as David Grossman) who sought to cope with the Holocaust, its aftermath and its impact on the generations that followed. Although some writers might have hesitated to use the Holocaust as a subject for literature at one time, this has changed. A stream of books has poured out in many lands. Some of the best known are noted in the accompanying box.

L I T H U A N I A

Largest of the Baltic States in northeastern Europe. At the beginning of WORLD WAR II, it had 3 million inhabitants, mainly farmers. Most were Catholics. The

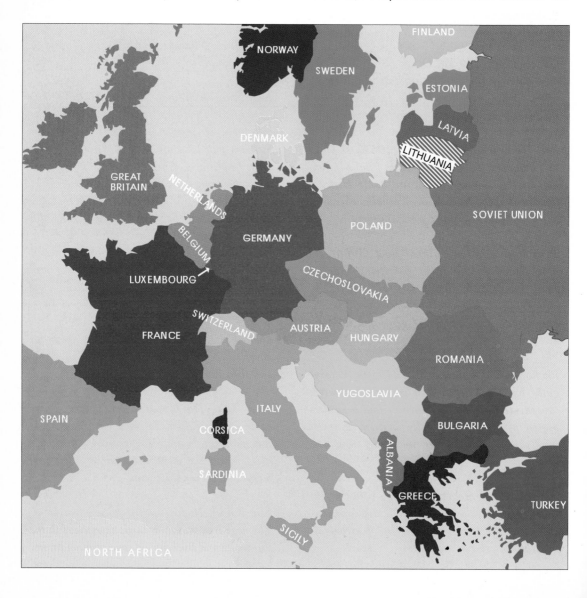

Jews being beaten by Lithuanians as German soldiers look on

250,000 JEWS were the country's largest ethnic minority. They worked mostly in business, industry, crafts, and the professions. The biggest Jewish communities were in the capital VILNA (Vilnius), KOVNO (Kaunas), and Shavli (Siauliai). There were also over 200 smaller communities. Almost all the communities had a synagogue and Hebrew and Yiddish schools. The rabbinic academies (*yeshivot*) in Lithuania were famous for their scholarship.

In the 1930s, the situation of the Jews worsened as a result of Nazi antisemitic PROPAGANDA. At this time, Jews became victims of physical attacks.

When communist SOVIET RUSSIA took over Lithuania in 1940, the Jews suffered more than the rest of the population from the economic changes. They were also affected by the banning of Hebrew education and the requirement to work on Sabbaths and festivals. The number of Jews exiled to Siberia was also proportionately greater than for the rest of the population. (It is ironic that these Jews were more fortunate in the long run since they were saved from the HOLOCAUST.) Despite all this, the Lithuanians accused the Jews of identifying with the Soviets and their hatred of the Jews grew.

When war broke out between GERMANY and Russia in June 1941, armed Lithuanians began to kill and plunder their Jewish neighbors even before the Germans arrived. Thousands of Jews fled to the interior of the Soviet Union. There they joined the Lithuanian Division of the Red Army and fought the Germans.

Within a few days of their invasion of Russia, the Germans conquered Lithuania and immediately ordered economic restrictions and made humiliating decrees regarding the Jews, such as wearing the Jewish BADGE. The EINSATZGRUPPEN carried out systematic killings of the Jews with the aim of destroying them completely. Lithuanian Jewry were the first victims of the mass murder, which became known as the "FINAL SOLUTION." The Nazis were assisted, often with enthusiasm, by Lithuanian soldiers, local police, students, teachers, and even priests. While the Germans were responsible for the overall planning, the preparations and supervision of the murders were in the hands of the Lithuanians. The Lithuanians rounded up the Jews, took them to killing sites, pushed them into prepared pits, and shot them. In some cases, the victims were forced to dig their own graves before being shot.

By the end of 1941, the great majority of Lithuanian Jews had been murdered. Those who remained were gathered into a number of closed GHETTOS in the larger cities. Some were employed in FORCED LABOR for the war effort, while others—such as the aged, women, and children—were put to death in nearby killing sites, such as PONARY near Vilna, FORT NINE near Kovno, and Kuzh near Shavli. A year of comparative quiet in the ghettos followed. Despite the restrictions and forced labor, the Jewish authorities in the ghettos succeeded in improving the living conditions. Cultural events were organized and a Jewish fighting UNDERGROUND came into being. Even so, the end was unavoidable.

The Vilna ghetto was liquidated in the fall of 1943. Most of its inhabitants were sent to CONCENTRATION CAMPS in ESTONIA. The survivors in the Kovno and Shavli ghettos were sent to concentration camps in Germany in the summer of 1944, shortly before the Red Army liberated Lithuania. Only 2,000 Jews survived in Lithuania, most of them by escaping to the forests and joining the PARTISANS. A minority was saved by non-Jews. Some survived the German camps. By the end of the war, 94 percent of the Jews of Lithuania had been killed, the highest percentage of any European country.

L   Ó   D   Z

Poland's second largest city. At the time of the German occupation in 1939, there were some 230,000 JEWS out of a total population of 665,000. Jews were involved largely in the textile industry, both as owners and as laborers. Lódz contained a variety of Jewish institutions, including the first Jewish high school in Russia (or POLAND), a large number of Orthodox and Chassidic educational institutions and many Zionist societies.

Lódz was occupied by the Germans on 8 September 1939 and was officially renamed Litzmannstadt. Almost immediately, persecution of the Jews began and soon ruined Jewish economic and social life. Lódz's substantial ethnic German community (10%) was organized to participate in these actions. In the following months, synagogues were destroyed, property was seized, Jews were forced to wear the yellow BADGE, travel was restricted and homes were taken over. In October 1939, the *Ältestenrat*, Council of Elders, was established with Mordechai Chaim RUMKOWSKI as its chairman.

While Lódz was not the first ghetto, it was the first place systematically set up as a closed ghetto. The idea of restricting Jews to a small compound and then exploiting them as a work force had al-

Bridge connecting two parts of the Lódz Ghetto. The road passing beneath was not part of the ghetto

ready been suggested by Hermann GÖRING as early as October 1938. However, the final fate of the Lódz ghetto was anticipated even before its establishment by police order on 8 February 1940 (see box). By the end of April of that year, 164,000 Jews were forced into an area of 1.5 square miles (4 square kilometers).

The Nazi plan for the ghetto targeted various goals: the exploitation of the ghetto population as slave laborers in factories; the deportation of as many Jews as possible; the confiscation of property; and the physical harassment of the population to cause a high rate of death by "natural causes." The loss of life to disease, cold and starvation was enormous.

On the Jewish side, the unfortunate task of implementing Nazi orders fell to Rumkowski and his council, a job which they were forced to do under penalty of death. Rumkowski carried this burden for five years until his deportation to AUSCHWITZ where he was killed. Rumkowski sought to limit deportations, to find occupation for the Jews in factories and protect their welfare. In spite of the difficulties, the Lódz ghetto was able to organize educational and cultural activities, as well as health care. There was even a Jewish ghetto police force.

The first wave of deportations from the Lódz ghetto began in December 1940 and continued un-

The establishment of the ghetto is naturally only an interim measure. When and how the ghetto and the city of Lódz will be purged of Jews is something I reserve for my exclusive decision. In any case, however, the final aim will be to burn this fraternity of pestilence to the end.

Friedrich Ubelhor, governor of the Kalisz-Lódz District, December 1939

til June 1942. From the beginning of January 1942, those deported were sent to the CHELMNO extermination camp. Another series of deportations came in September 1942, reducing the population of the ghetto to less than 90,000. The strong underground movement was unable to take any effective action against the deportations. By 1 September 1944, the date of the liquidation of the Lódz ghetto, the population had dwindled to 77,000, all of whom were deported to Auschwitz. Some 800 Jews, part of a "mopping-up" force, were liberated by the Soviet Army before their German captors could use the graves which had already been prepared for them.

Selling books in the Lódz Ghetto

LUBETKIN, ZIVIA

(1914–1976) A founder of the JEWISH FIGHTING ORGANI-ZATION in WORLD WAR II. Lubetkin became active in a Zionist youth movement in Eastern Europe when World War II broke out. As soon as she could, she fled to WARSAW, where she became a founding member of the Antifascist Bloc. It was the first partially successful attempt to set up an armed underground in Warsaw.

In July 1942, when the deportation of Jews from Warsaw to the death camps was moving at an intensive pace, Lubetkin helped found the Jewish Fighting Organization—the ZOB. She became a member of its political arm and of the liaison committee between the ZOB and the Jewish Socialist Bund. Lubetkin fought in the brief January 1943 uprising in the Warsaw ghetto and again in the WARSAW GHETTO UPRISING that broke out on 19 April 1943. On 10 May, she escaped by way of the sewers and remained in hiding until the Red Army took Warsaw. She emerged to take part in the Polish Warsaw uprising in 1944.

After the war Lubetkin became active in survivor circles and the BERIHA, an organization devoted to bringing Jews from Europe to PALESTINE. She reached Palestine herself in 1946 and helped found the Ghetto Fighters' Kibbutz and museum (see GHETTO FIGHTERS' HOUSE). She married another former underground leader, Yitzhak ZUCKERMAN.

Zivia Lubetkin giving evidence at the Eichmann Trial, Jerusalem, 1961

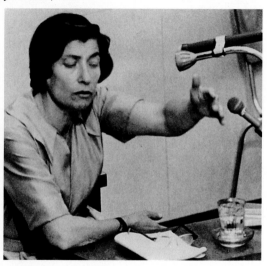

LUBLIN

City in POLAND. On the eve of WORLD WAR II, Lublin was a center of Jewish cultural and political life. About 40,000 JEWS lived there, out of a total population of 120,000.

On 18 September 1939, German forces occupied the city. The Germans immediately seized Jews for FORCED LABOR and confiscated Jewish property. In November 1939, Jews were ordered to wear the Jewish BADGE, and their movements were restricted.

The city of Lublin was part of the greater Lublin region. This area was chosen by the Nazis as a "reservation"—really a dumping ground—for Jews from other parts of Poland. This program was called the NISKO AND LUBLIN PLAN. As part of this plan, 6,300 Polish Jews were sent to Lublin by February 1940. The program ended the following April.

The Germans established a Jewish Council (JUDEN-RAT) on 25 January 1940. It had 24 members from different Jewish political parties. Like other Jewish Councils throughout Poland, it had to balance trying to make life as tolerable as possible for Jews and following German demands. In the case of forced labor, the Germans kidnapped Jews for labor off the streets if the Judenrat did not meet the quota. The Judenrat tried to keep as many Jews as possible working in factories inside the city. However, in the summer of 1940, they were ordered to provide large quotas of Jews for LABOR CAMPS near the Soviet border. The Judenrat obeyed because they feared what would happen if they refused. This caused tension between the Judenrat and the Jews of Lublin.

In March 1941, the Nazis began to "resettle" large numbers of Jews from Lublin to smaller communities in Poland. At the same time, a GHETTO was established. The 34,000 Jews left in Lublin were crowded into a small area. They were not allowed to leave unless they had work permits. Conditions in the ghetto were terrible. A typhus epidemic broke out there in the summer of 1941 and starvation was widespread.

Lublin was the headquarters for AKTION REINHARD—the Nazis' systematic program for deporting Jews to DEATH CAMPS. The MAJDANEK death camp was located just outside the city. Jews from Lublin were among the first to be deported to the BELZEC death camp at a rate of 1,400 a day—beginning on 17 March 1942.

Deportation from the Lublin Ghetto

Selections for DEPORTATION took place at assembly points throughout the ghetto. Jews with work per- mits were at first exempt from deportations (though not their families). To avoid deportation, about 500

German soldier cutting the beard of a Jew in the Lublin Ghetto

Jews escaped into hiding outside the ghetto. Almost all were caught and immediately killed.

The first deportation AKTION ("operation") in Lublin ended on 20 April 1942. In less than a month, 30,000 Jews were sent to their deaths at Belzec. The remaining 4,000 Jews were forcibly moved to Majdan Tatarski, a suburb of Lublin, which was made into a "small ghetto." Many of its inhabitants were murdered soon after their arrival. During September and October 1942, 3,800 people were deported to Majdanek. Jews continued to be murdered throughout 1943.

The Nazis retreated from Lublin in the summer of 1944. No Jews remained alive. Soon after the city's liberation, Lublin became an assembly point for Jewish REFUGEES in the area, as well as Jewish PARTISANS. Since Lublin was one of the first cities freed from German control, it became the temporary capital of Poland (until the liberation of WARSAW in January 1945), as well as the center of community life for Jewish survivors. Under the communists, Jewish life in Lublin all but disappeared. Today, few Jews live there.

LUTZ, CARL

(1895–1975) Swiss diplomat who saved thousands of Jews in BUDAPEST. After serving in PALESTINE, (Israel) he was appointed vice-consul in Budapest in January 1942. Lutz was in charge of the Swiss Embassy's foreign interests department. Since he also represented British interests, Lutz came into contact with Moshe (Miklos) Krausz, head of the Jewish Agency's Palestine Office in Budapest, who handled the emigration certificates to Palestine that were sent to HUNGARY.

At that time, Britain was responsible for emigration to Palestine. In June 1944, with Lutz's help, Krausz obtained British agreement to declare all certificate holders potential citizens of Palestine. At the same time, he obtained the Hungarian authorities' permission to allow these people to emigrate. In addition, it was agreed that the certificates were valid not only for the person named in them but for their families too. Thus, a Collective Passport was prepared, valid for 7,500 Jews. Krausz also persuaded the Weisz family, wealthy Jewish glass manufacturers, to allow the Swiss Embassy to use their

town office, the "Glass House." The Glass House became the Emigration Office of the Swiss Embassy's Department for Foreign Interests. With the full knowledge of Lutz, but of no one else at the Embassy, this place became the center of rescue and of the relief activities of the Zionist YOUTH MOVEMENTS. From here Letters of Protection (*Schutzpässe*) were issued to some 70,000 Jews. These documents bore no official signature—just a forged rubber stamp or forged signature. When confronted with these passports, however, Lutz never denied that the signatures were authentic. Tens of thousands of falsified papers were distributed by Zionist youths from this office. Lutz's action was followed by some other diplomats, notably Raoul WALLENBERG of the Swedish Embassy.

Not all of these documents were accepted by the Nazis and did not save their holders. On 15 October 1944, the pro-Nazi ARROW CROSS took over power in Budapest and the mass deportations of Jews to AUSCHWITZ began. The Glass House and the adjoining vacant premises of the Hungarian Football Association housed some 3,000 Jews under Lutz's protection. All but six survived.

After the war, Lutz, returned to SWITZERLAND, retired and lived on a meager income. He was one of the first to be recognized as a RIGHTEOUS AMONG THE NATIONS by YAD VASHEM.

LUXEMBOURG

Small country in western Europe. About 3,500 JEWS lived there on the eve of WORLD WAR II—30 percent of them refugees, who had arrived since 1933. The total population of Luxembourg was about 300,000. Luxembourg was invaded by the Germans on 10 May 1940, when they also invaded BELGIUM, the NETHERLANDS and FRANCE. After two and a half months of military administration, a Nazi civil administration was set up.

In the early stages of the occupation, many Jews fled to Belgium and France. Some returned shortly afterward, when things seemed to have calmed down. On 5 September 1940, however, the NUREMBERG LAWS were activated, and confiscation of Jewish property began in Luxembourg. Many Jewish businesses were ARYANIZED and Jewish-owned farms and lands were turned over to local people of German

Deportation of the Jews of Luxembourg, September 1942

origin. A number of laws that restricted the freedom of movement of Jews were later passed. Hundreds of Jews were assigned to FORCED LABOR. In September 1941, Jews were forced to wear yellow BADGES. Between August 1940 and May 1941, 16 groups of Jews—most of them youngsters, but also the leadership of the community—were forced to move to France and Portugal. By October 1941, 80 percent of the Jews left in the country were over the age of 50.

In August 1941, the Nazis started to assemble Jews in a Jesuit monastery. From there they were deported to the east. On 16 October 1941, the first DEPORTATION, of 324 Jews to the LÓDZ GHETTO, took place. This was followed by another 8 deportations; the last one—with 674 Jews—was on 28 September 1943. Of the prewar Jewish population of Luxembourg 1,945 died. Many were sent directly to DEATH CAMPS; some were sent to other countries and from there to their deaths. Only 36 survived the deportations. Luxembourg was liberated from the Nazis in September 1944 and became an important financial center of Europe.

L V O V

(formerly called Lemberg) An historic city in East Galicia now in the UKRAINE Republic. Prior to WORLD WAR II it was under Polish rule, but was a place of dispute between Poles and Ukrainians. Ukrainian nationalist activity was most widespread there. In 1939, Lvov had a Jewish population of 100,000 out of a total of 340,000. It was the third largest Jewish center in POLAND (after WARSAW and LODZ).

Lvov was occupied by Soviet forces three weeks after the outbreak of the war, and was soon annexed by Soviet Russia. Meanwhile, its population was swelled by 100,000 Jews fleeing the German-occupied part of Poland. The Soviets closed all non-Communist Jewish institutions, and restricted their business life. This caused many to plunge into poverty. Wealthy Jews and those suspected of Zionist or other "anti-Communist" activity, were deported to Siberia.

Lvov fell to the Germans on 30 June 1941. The murder of Jews began immediately. For four days, Jews were hunted down and robbed, tortured and

A Jew being beaten and dragged along the streets of Lvov

killed. This bloodbath claimed the lives of 4,000 Jews and was conducted mostly by Ukrainians assisted by Germans and criminals released from jail. The Germans filmed the slaughter, and a copy has survived. A second pogrom was unleashed in which 2,000 Jews lost their lives.

A ghetto was established November 1941, and thousands of Jews were killed in the process of being moved there. A JUDENRAT was formed to convey the demands of the Germans to the Jewish community. Its first leader was shot for refusing to hand over Jews to the Germans. In March 1942, an AKTION was carried out in which 15,000 Jews were deported to the death camp at BELZEC. In August, 50,000 Jews were sent to Belzec. This was followed by a series of deportations, including some to a camp established within Lvov itself, called JANÓWSKA. In January 1943, the ghetto was converted into a labor camp. All Jews unable to work were killed. However, between May and June 1943, even those who had been working were murdered. By that time, an underground movement had been established. When Germans and Ukrainians came to murder Jews, some resisted and a number of Nazis were killed. Most escape attempts ended in failure, in part due to the hostility of the local population.

When Lvov was liberated in 1944, several hundred Jews were found who had survived the war by hiding with gentiles, or because they possessed papers "proving" they were Aryans.

index

Darkened numbers indicate an entry on the subject in this volume